THE
HOLY SECRET

Ask What - Context/meaning
Ask Why - word/order/tone
Look for patterns - word/linguistic structures/repetitions
      themes/parrell/
What Reveal Abt Christ/Atonement
How is about me -

THE
HOLY SECRET

JAMES L. FERRELL

DESERET
BOOK

SALT LAKE CITY, UT

Library of Congress Cataloging-in-Publication Data

Ferrell, James L.
The holy secret / James L. Ferrell.
   p. cm.
  Includes bibliographical references.
  ISBN-13: 978-1-59038-718-4 (hardcover : alk. paper)
  1. Christian life—Mormon authors—Miscellanea. 2. Church of Jesus Christ of Latter-day Saints—Doctrines—Miscellanea. I. Title.
  BX8656.F47 2008
  289.3'32—dc22   2007047891

Printed in the United States of America
Publishers Printing, Salt Lake City, UT

10 9 8 7 6 5 4 3 2 1

"I am able to make you holy."

—D&C 60:7

CONTENTS

CONTENTS

PART III
LOVING THE HOLY TEMPLE

PREFACE

I believe that many today carry a secret: we do not love what we have been commanded to love; we do not love what is holy. While we might reverence things that are deemed holy—the temple, for example, and the scriptures, and the Sabbath—we do not love them. Not really. Not with our whole souls.

I want to be careful not to be misunderstood. While I know that I, at times, have carried this secret, I do not presume the same about any other particular person. But our actions as a *people*—both as members of The Church of Jesus Christ of Latter-day Saints and as part of the larger Christian population—suggest that as a body of believers we do not love what is holy. Our temples, for example, are not as busy as they would be if we loved being there; the pages of our scriptures are not as worn as they would be if we feasted upon their words; our stores are not as empty or our chapels as filled as they would be if we truly loved the Lord's holy day. While many among us surely cherish and love holiness, our lives suggest that many more of us do not. At least, not all of the time.

Why does this matter? It matters because the scriptures teach that if we are to enjoy eternal life in the hereafter, we must be sanctified from sin and enjoy the words of eternal life in the here and now.[1] If we do not enjoy holiness here, we will not have the opportunity to experience it there.

So what is to be done? Why are we not passionately in love with what is holy? What is holding us back and keeping us away? What is keeping us from holiness?

This book is the story of a keeper of this secret who unexpectedly begins to love what is holy. The scriptures, the Sabbath, and the temple come alive for him. He discovers a joy for these vessels of holiness that before had been only theoretical. He discovers as well, to his great surprise, that a love for what is holy transforms his love for life itself. Petty grievances, ongoing squabbles, and grudges long held are washed from his heart as he begins to apply the cleansing agent of holiness.

These revelations come to him, as they can to us, as he embarks on a journey of discovery. It is a journey in the scriptures, on the Sabbath, and through the temple—a journey that begins with a conversation about holiness with someone who didn't always, but has learned to, love it.

PART I

LOVING THE
HOLY SCRIPTURES

I

AWAKENING

Michael Nowak steered his car along the winding, tree-lined streets of Stamford, Connecticut, not going anywhere in particular. He had left church early that Sabbath morning, driven from the building by a talk that had pricked him to the core. Although he didn't have anything major to hide or to run from, the remarks that day had awakened Michael to a weakness. He was carrying a secret even he usually didn't know. But he knew it today, and the realization made him shudder.

Brother Albert Kishler, a still spry seventy-year-old who had lost his wife to cancer just six months earlier, had been the speaker. A grocery man by trade, Brother Kishler possessed an easy way with others that made him a favorite among both old and young. Since his wife's death, he had returned to work two days a week, and although he no longer managed the store, you wouldn't be able to convince any of the long-time patrons of that. He was something of an institution in the area, among Church members and nonmembers alike.

Michael pondered Brother Kishler's words as he wound his way beneath the canopies of Connecticut maples and oaks. "If I don't love what is holy in this life," Brother Kishler had said, "then I will not like holiness in the next. My attitude about what is holy here and now tells me where I am heading in the then and there."

Michael had been fine to that point, but then Brother Kishler got specific.

"The holy scriptures," he declared, "do we love them? Do we, as the Lord said to Adam, 'enjoy the words of eternal life in this world' so that we might 'enjoy eternal life in the world to come'?[2] Do we curl up with the scriptures, yearning to read them, or do we mostly avoid them, picking up a thought here or there in meetings we attend? We mustn't kid ourselves. What is dull to us today remains dull to us tomorrow. If our souls don't yearn to understand and study the Lord's words here, we will not suddenly begin to yearn for them upon our passing from mortality. Today is the day appointed for us to prepare to meet God.[3] How are we preparing, brothers and sisters? Are we learning to love his holy words, as recorded in the holy scriptures?

"And," he had continued, "do we love the holy temple—

that sacred space that is the Lord's house on earth? Do we long to be there and to attend as often as possible? Do we love holiness to that degree? Or do we rather look forward to other activities and places?

"And the holy Sabbath," he added, "do we, from our hearts, reverence the holiness of this day? Do we delight in resting from worldly concerns and cares? Do we yearn for the Lord's rest? Do we love the holy Sabbath, brothers and sisters? Do we love what is holy?"

Beginning to feel pressed in by the implications of these words, Michael found himself turning for escape into the eastbound entrance of Merritt Parkway, a picturesque highway that cuts through the Connecticut greenery from the New York border. *I enjoy the Sabbath,* he defended himself. He had to admit, however, that the other questions indicted him. He knew, despite the testimonies he had borne to the contrary, that he didn't really love the scriptures. He read them on a semi-regular basis, but more out of duty than anything else. He didn't feel like he got much out of them anymore.

As for the temple, he just didn't enjoy going. The repetition, ritual, and symbolism bored him anymore, and he found that he spent most of his time while there complaining to himself about how none of it seemed relevant to his daily life. Busy as a young Wall Street lawyer, his schedule gave him a ready excuse; he hadn't been to the temple in months.

These were all secrets, of course—secrets Michael was

pretty sure were unknown even to his wife, Angie. He was a temple-recommend-holding, tithe-paying, lesson-preparing, testimony-bearing member. Usually, this seemed like enough, and he comforted himself with the knowledge that he was doing what he'd been commanded to do. However, as his car hummed eastward on the Merritt, his soul ached with another bit of knowledge: that despite all he had been doing, he was failing at something fundamental. Where the Lord dwelt all was holiness—"Holiness" being one of his names.[4] Michael now was worried about what that might mean.

"I am getting on in years," Brother Kishler had said near the end of his remarks. "Too old, perhaps, to be distracted by the glitz and glamour of this world. But I am grateful in my old age to love holiness. Those of you who know me best know that it wasn't always so." He then paused to collect himself, and in the honest, heartfelt silence that followed, emotion moistened the hearts in the room.

"But I thank the Lord for his loving kindness toward me, for his mercy and for his grace. And I thank him as well for my dear Helen," he said, his voice beginning to wobble. "She was holy, brothers and sisters." He wiped at his cheek. "If I ever hope to be with her again, I must love what she loved. And I believe that the scriptures, the Sabbath, and the temple—those mediums of holiness extended into this unholy world—are what I need in order to prepare. May we learn to love them, brothers and sisters, so that we might one day live with those we dearly love, and those who dearly love us."

Mediums of holiness, Michael repeated to himself as he drove. One of the implications of Brother Kishler's talk was that the Lord has extended into this fallen realm a way for us to learn to love what he loves, and to therefore be able to live where he lives. Those who learn to love these "mediums of holiness" become holy themselves, which is the sanctification necessary to live again with God.

But I don't love them, Michael muttered, shaking his head despairingly. *Brother Kishler is right. I don't love what is holy.*

Over the next half hour or so, Michael wrestled with this insight, alternately denying it and recognizing it anew, until he finally arrived at a question: *Then what can I do about it? I've been going to church all my adult life. If I don't love the scriptures and the temple by now, what could possibly help me at this point?*

He didn't know, and the dearth of ideas depressed him.

"What can I do, Lord?" he finally cried heavenward. "How can I learn to love what is holy?"

He drove on in silence, listening.

Then, with the faintest of hope, he veered off the next exit.

He needed to see Brother Kishler.

CURIOSITY

Michael pulled into Brother Kishler's driveway some thirty minutes after church would have ended. He glanced at his watch: 1:30 P.M. Michael's wife, Angie, and their two children, four-year-old Hayden and two-year-old Erika, were in Seattle visiting Angie's family. He would need to check in with them later in the day, but for now he had the afternoon free.

He parked his car next to the well-manicured hedge that lined the far side of the driveway and made his way to the front door. Brother Kishler lived in a meticulously cared-for white clapboard colonial home that was nearly two hundred years old. Dark green shutters adorned the sides of the home's many windows. Flower boxes lined the bottom of the first-floor windows and the multicolored impatiens that peeked above the edges of the boxes gave the home a cheery, inviting look.

Majestic pines lined the property on both sides of the house, and an ancient, ten-story maple sheltered much of the front yard from the sweltering July sun.

He is certainly keeping busy, Michael said to himself as he admired the state of the yard. Michael's own townhome, although upscale, included only a tiny mow-strip that was maintained by the homeowners' association. While Angie had been hinting for the past year that their young children needed a yard, Michael had so far delayed any serious talk of home purchase, partly because he had hated lawn-upkeep as a child and the memory had solidified nearly into a phobia in adulthood. Or so he liked to think; a psychological condition gave him cover that mere slothfulness did not.

As Michael was about to knock on the door, Brother Kishler turned into the driveway. He pulled quickly to a stop and sprang from the car. "Hello, Michael," he greeted. "What a pleasant surprise!"

Brother Kishler was a good six foot three inches tall but stood with a bit of a stoop, as if embarrassed to look down on anyone. His head was perpetually bowed, his glasses riding low on his nose, so that when he looked at others, he typically peered at them over the top of the rims. Over the years, the pull of his facial muscles to raise his gaze up and over the tops of his glasses had left thoughtful creases across his forehead. For the same reason, his eyebrows seemed perpetually raised, a look that made him seem friendly and interested. As he approached Michael, he walked with a hint of pigeon-toe, which added a level of vulnerability. Overall, his appearance put one at ease.

"Thank you, Brother Kishler. I'm sorry to be bothering you on your Sunday afternoon."

Brother Kishler waved the comment off. "Not at all. It's lonely in this old house. I welcome the company. You'll come in, won't you?" He smiled warmly at Michael.

This was precisely what Michael had wanted, but he hesitated, not wanting to seem forward.

"Of course you will," Brother Kishler said, sensing the mock reserve. "I wouldn't allow you to leave even if you wanted," he winked.

He turned to the door, fumbling in his pocket for his keys. "Oh," he said, half turning his head while he was unbolting the door, "and call me Al. A life among produce and dairy doesn't lend to formality."

Michael smiled. "Okay," he answered, not yet comfortable enough to reference him by name, even with the invitation.

"There we are," Albert said, as he opened the door. "Please, come in."

Michael stepped through the doorway. "Are you alone today?" Albert asked.

"Angie and the kids are in Seattle visiting her parents," Michael answered.

"So it's just us two lonely men, then, huh?"

"Yeah," Michael laughed. "I guess so."

"Can I get you something to drink? You must be thirsty."

"Uh, sure," Michael answered. "Water would be fine. Thank you."

"Then lemonade it is," Albert smiled. "Yellow or pink?"

"Uh, yellow would be great. Thanks."

Albert nodded. "I'll be right back. Make yourself at home."

Michael looked around at what looked more like a library than a typical sitting or living room. Rich walnut shelves lined the walls, each of them bursting with books. Here and there a framed picture broke up the stacks—mostly pictures of Al and Helen through the years. *But no pictures of children,* Michael noted. A bronze Christus stood watch over the room from the mantel over the fireplace.

"Here we are," Albert said, as he carried a tray with a pitcher of lemonade and a couple of ice-filled glasses into the room. "Please, make yourself at home," he said, nodding toward the leather sofa. "Best seat in the house."

"Thank you, uh, Al," Michael said as he relaxed onto the couch.

"Certainly. Here you go," he said, handing Michael a glass and filling it with lemonade.

"So," he said, as he sat down in the chair facing Michael, "to what do I owe this pleasure?"

Michael took his glass down to his lap, holding it with both hands. Despite his time in the car, he hadn't thought to prepare a way into the conversation.

"I have some questions," he finally managed to say. "About your talk."

Albert's eyebrows lifted. "You didn't like it?"

"Oh, no, I was moved by it actually. It moved me right out of the building, in fact."

"Did I offend you?"

"No, no, not at all," Michael said, shaking his head vigorously. "You didn't say anything that could offend. But I *would* say I came away troubled."

"I see. So I did offend you."

"No," Michael laughed. "You've just gotten me to thinking, that's all."

"Dangerous thing, that."

"Thinking?"

"Yes."

Michael chuckled to himself. "Maybe so," he agreed. "But that's why I'm here. I need the benefit of your thinking."

"*My* thinking?" Albert asked. "You're the young prodigy lawyer at Cravath, Swaine, and—" Albert paused. "What was the other name?"

"Moore. Cravath, Swaine, and Moore."

"Wall Street firm, isn't it?"

Michael nodded.

"And you want the thoughts of this high school diploma'd grocery man?"

"Where the gospel is concerned," Michael answered with no hesitation, "I am afraid I'm still working on my equivalency degree. That is what you made me realize today. I'm here to learn."

"From me?"

"Yes."

Albert looked down at his glass, thinking. "What is it you think you need to learn?"

Michael hesitated. Unthinkingly, he almost mentioned the unadulterated truth—that he didn't really enjoy the scriptures and felt no desire to attend the temple. But he had spent his whole life playing the part of the active member—the scripture reader, the temple believer—and before the words escaped his lips, his reflexes invited him to make a more acceptable pronouncement: "I—" he began, "I want to know what you know." That was safe. And true, as far as it went.

Albert's lips flattened. "I'm afraid I can't help you then," he answered.

Michael was perplexed. "But you clearly know things I don't," he responded.

Albert smiled. "You see all these books?" he asked, as he gestured to the shelves around them.

"Yes. Pretty impressive," Michael answered.

"There are two things I'd like you to know about them," Albert said.

"Okay," Michael answered in anticipation.

"The first is that I've read them all."

Michael looked around—biographies on Washington, Adams, Lincoln, and Churchill, the plays of William Shakespeare, the writings of Dante, Goethe, Dickens, Plato, Aristotle, Aquinas, C. S. Lewis, DeTocqueville, weighty works such as *The Rise and Fall of the Roman Empire* and *The History of the Church*. Formidable titles in all directions.

"Wow, that's quite a feat," Michael said.

"Yes, a feat that makes possible the second thing I'd like you to know about these books."

"Yes? What is that?"

"That I remember almost nothing I have read from them."

Michael's brow furrowed. "You mean they've been a waste?"

"That's not what I said. I said that I can remember very little of what I have read out of their pages."

"Then they've been a waste. That's what you're saying."

"No, that's *not* what I'm saying."

Albert stood up and pulled a book from the shelf. He opened it and began to caress the pages. Michael could tell he loved the book—reverenced it, even.

"I've learned something very important from these books,"

he said. "For the most part, however, it hasn't been what's been written on their pages."

Michael was befuddled. "Then what? What have you learned from them?"

"They cured me of the temptation of thinking that what I need is just one more bit of information, one more piece of knowledge, one more book."

Michael wasn't sure what was left standing by this cure. "Then what? What did they do for you?"

"They helped me to become curious," he said, looking straight at Michael. "They taught me how to ask questions. They taught me, and continue to teach me, how to learn."

"Can you teach me that, then?" Michael asked.

Albert looked at him. "That depends."

"On what?"

"On you."

3

QUESTIONS

Good. Because I'm willing."

"You're willing to have a conversation?"

Michael was delighted by the implication—that Albert would spend time with him and help him. "Certainly. I'd be honored."

"Then let me introduce you to your conversation partners."

At that, Albert walked toward the Christus and pulled down two large books that were stacked on the mantel just to the right of the statue. "Here," he said, extending them to Michael. "Your companions."

Michael took hold of the books—a large leather-covered Bible and Book of Mormon. "My companions?" he asked, looking curiously at Albert.

"Yes. You didn't fall in love with your wife by having a conversation with someone else, did you?"

"Well, no, but—"

"No conversation with me will make you fall in love with the scriptures either. You need to converse with them directly. If you do, you'll fall deeply in love with them. I promise."

"But I've been doing that all my life," Michael protested. "That's the problem. I've been reading them all my life but I don't really enjoy them, and I'm worried about what that means."

Albert nodded. "I didn't say to read them, Michael. I said to have a conversation with them. There's a difference."

"I'm not sure I understand."

Albert smiled and took his seat. "Just notice what's going on right now," he said. "We are engaging each other with questions, comments, and objections; we are in *conversation*. But imagine how different our experience together would be if one of us just sat here and waited for the other to speak. Do you think that would be as interesting and engaging as this is proving to be?"

"Probably not, no"

"I'm guessing that *that* is your problem, Michael. You have not been engaging the scriptures in conversation but have been waiting for them to teach you; you have turned them into a monologue."

"But they *are* a monologue. The prophets who wrote them are dead."

"Yes, but their words aren't—unless we allow them to be."

Michael frowned. "You're saying that's what I'm doing—I'm allowing the prophets' words to be dead to me?"

"Actually, Michael, that's what *you* have said. You said that you don't enjoy reading the scriptures. That means, I take it, that they don't invigorate you; you do not find them enlivening. Am I right?"

Michael nodded hesitantly.

"Then they are dead to you."

Michael had to admit the truth of that. "But I don't want them to be," he lamented. "That's why I need your help."

"If you don't want the scriptures to be dead to you," Albert responded, "may I suggest that you stop being dead to them."

"Okay, then how?" Michael pleaded. "I don't even understand a lot of what I read in them," he volunteered—a truth he had never admitted to anyone. "We've been studying the Old Testament in Sunday School, for example, and frankly, a lot of it is impenetrable."

"Then you have lots of opportunities to ask questions," Albert responded.

"I'm not one to speak much in class," Michael replied.

"Oh, I wasn't talking about asking questions in class," Albert said, waving his hand in front of him. "I was talking about asking questions of the book itself."

"Of the book? Of the Old Testament, you mean?"

"If that is the work of scripture you are having a conversation with, yes," Albert nodded.

Michael's eyes lit up with understanding. "Oh, I get it. By having a conversation with the scriptures, you mean I need to be asking questions as I'm reading."

"Among other things," Albert nodded.

"Like what, then?" Michael asked. "What questions? What other things?"

"Do you have time?" Albert asked, glancing at the clock on the mantel.

"I'm alone, remember? I have as much time as you need."

"Very well, then," Albert smiled, "let's have a conversation."

4

ASK "WHAT?"

Let's start with what you probably know best—The Book of
Mormon. Then we can move to what you should know
just as well, to what I myself have grown to love with my whole
soul, the Old Testament.

"But we'll ease into it," he added, seeming to sense
Michael's unease at the mention of that formidable book.

"Thanks," Michael said, half in jest.

"If you will," Albert invited, "turn in the Book of Mormon
to the book of 1 Nephi, the second chapter and fifteenth verse."

Yes, an area I know all too well, Michael thought to himself
as he turned to the verse, *what with all the times I've begun the
book.*

His eyes fell upon 1 Nephi 2:15: "And my father dwelt in a

tent." He chuckled. "Did you mean something else? Maybe verse 14 or 16?"

Albert grinned. "No, I meant verse 15."

"And my father dwelt in a tent?" Michael double checked.

"Yes."

"Okay," Michael responded tepidly.

"One of the great verses in the scriptures," Albert glowed.

"One of the shortest, I'll give you that," Michael joked. "But best?" He raised his eyebrows in doubt.

"Actually, if you enter into conversation with this verse," Albert countered, "you will find it to be exceedingly long."

Michael was skeptical. He was beginning to wonder whether coming to see Brother Kishler had been such a good idea.

"Here's a question I'd like you to ask of that verse," Albert said: "Ask: *What?* In other words, what's the context? Or what's the meaning of the words?"

"Well, the words are pretty plain."

"Are they? Then what about the word, *dwelt?* After all, it could have been *slept,* or *stayed,* or any number of other words, but instead the word is *dwelt.* What might that imply?"

Michael paused as he considered the question. "Hmm. It implies a period of time, doesn't it."

"Go on," Albert invited.

"Well, a word like *slept* or *stayed* would make his stay seem more transitory. But *dwelt* has a ring of permanence to it. It sounds like they stayed awhile."

"And did they?" Albert asked.

Michael hadn't ever considered the question. "I guess I don't know," he finally answered.

"Then let's back up and look at the context," Albert said. "What's going on here? Why is Lehi now dwelling in a tent?"

"Because the Lord commanded him to leave Jerusalem."

"Why?"

"Because it was soon going to be destroyed by the Babylonians."

"Okay," Albert nodded. "What else do we know about the context?"

Michael puzzled for a moment.

"Go back to the first verse of chapter 1."

"I know that one by heart," Michael said. "I, Nephi," he began, "having been born of goodly parents—"

"*Goodly?*" Albert interrupted. "What does *goodly* mean?"

"That they were good people, that they were righteous," Michael answered.

"It seems like that, doesn't it?" Albert said.

"You're saying that that's wrong?" Michael started.

"Oh, we soon learn they were good people—their subsequent actions demonstrate that. I'm just not convinced that is the primary thing Nephi was trying to tell us when he described them as *goodly*."

Michael leaned forward, his face creased with interest. "Then what?"

"Well," Albert began, "where might we look for an answer?"

"In a dictionary?" Michael wondered.

"Perhaps," Albert nodded. "Go ahead and look it up. The dictionary is there in the reference section," he said signaling to the wall opposite the fireplace. "Third shelf down."

Michael walked over to the shelf and took down a thick, well-worn dictionary. Its yellowed pages betrayed its age. Michael turned to "goodly," where he read the following.

good·ly (good´lē) *adj*. 1. Of pleasing appearance; comely. 2. Somewhat large; considerable: *a goodly sum.*

"That doesn't seem to fit," he said to Albert. "I don't think Nephi was saying his parents were pleasing in appearance or considerable. Maybe this dictionary is too old."

"More likely too new," Albert countered. "Something from closer to the time Joseph Smith translated the book might be helpful. Notice, however, that *virtuous* or the like—the meaning normally attributed to this word in this verse—isn't included in the list of possible definitions. Before you dismiss the listed definitions—*of pleasing appearance,* and *considerable*—let's reread the verse with them in mind."

Michael began reciting again: "I, Nephi, having been born of good-looking parents." He laughed. "That can't be right.

There's no way he would start the book that way, even if it were true."

He began again: "I, Nephi, having been born of considerable parents." He screwed up his face in dislike. "That doesn't sound right either."

"Keep going," Albert prodded.

"With what?"

"With the verse—using *considerable*."

"I, Nephi," Michael began again, "having been born of considerable parents, therefore I was taught somewhat in all the learning of my father—"

"Notice the word *therefore*," Albert interrupted once more. "What does it mean?"

"That what follows the word is a result of what preceded it," Michael answered.

"The clarity of a lawyer," Albert smiled, appreciatively.

"Sometimes we're paid for our ability to be obtuse," Michael chuckled back.

"Yes, but you have to have deep clarity in order to know how to make yourself unclear, don't you?" Albert cracked.

Michael laughed as he thought of the flowery "legalese" that bloated so many contracts and court filings.

"So yes," Albert continued, "what follows the *therefore* is somehow the result of what precedes it. So think about it: Does being taught in all the learning of one's father follow from one's father being *virtuous,* which is the way we normally read the verse?"

Michael frowned in contemplation. "It might," he finally answered. "A righteous person would be more likely to want to educate his children."

"But what if he didn't have the wherewithal to do it?" Albert questioned. "We're talking about ancient times here, when most people survived by the sweat of their brow. Extensive education was not the norm for most in those days— even among those you might think of as righteous. So righteousness itself doesn't seem to have a clear causal relationship with education."

Michael considered that. "I see your point. So where does that leave us?"

"With *considerable,*" Albert answered. "Think about it. What about the possibility that Lehi was somehow *considerable*—considerably wealthy or well-to-do, for example, as we know from later events that he was; might the wealth of one's parents have an impact on whether a child has an opportunity to be taught in all the learning of his father?"

That made good sense to Michael, especially in the context of ancient times. "Yes, it very well could," he answered.

"One way to check this reading of *goodly,*" Albert continued, "would be to compare it against other times the word is used in the scriptures. It turns out that the word appears thirty-nine times in scriptural writings. You might try looking up those references and seeing the ways the word is normally used. When you do that, I think you will find that it is most often used to describe something as impressive, high in station, abundant, or of considerable size or quality—all of which, when applied to Lehi, would suggest that Nephi is trying to tell us that he was taught in all the learning of his father on account of his father's high station and wealth."

Albert paused and eyed Michael. "Which brings us," he said, "to a second question that invites us into conversation with the scriptures: 'Why?'"

5

WONDER "WHY?"

Why *what?*" Michael asked.

"Why, for example," Albert responded, "did Nephi start the book the way he did and not some other way—especially if the book essentially begins with a mention of his parents' good station or wealth? Or why did he bother to inform us in chapter 2 that his 'father dwelt in a tent'? And why did he say *dwelt* instead of some other word? Why? Why? Why? The *why?* question is a great conversation starter."

Michael mulled that over for a moment. "Okay then," he said, "why *did* he start the book that way?"

"Don't ask me," Albert answered. "Ask the book."

Michael furrowed his brow in consternation.

"The book won't talk to you, no," Albert said, guessing Michael's mind, "but it *will* open up for you if you keep asking questions of it. It will inspire a conversation within you."

Michael remained silent, still perplexed.

"When your wife Angie is talking to you, Michael, do you listen only to her words?"

For a moment, this question jolted him from his thinking about the scriptures. "I guess I'm not sure what you mean. What else would I listen to but her words?"

"How about her tone of voice?" Albert asked. "Or her inflection? Or how about the words she chooses *not* to say? Do you ever read anything into her partial or perhaps even total silence?"

Silence. That was a topic he and Angie knew too well. Whenever she felt unappreciated, she clammed up and said nothing. The silence spoke volumes, of course. When she wasn't speaking to him, Michael knew she was feeling mistreated and taken for granted. And it irked him, because he knew that she was accusing him by her silence—accusing him of something he felt was undeserved. He usually responded with silence of his own, and the chill between them sometimes lasted for days.

"You're right," Michael said. "Silence carries a message."

"So you find meaning in silence?"

"Yes."

"And in tone?"

Michael nodded.

"So notice," Albert said, "in our daily lives we don't for a moment presume that the messages around us consist only in what is being said on the surface. We are always asking why—why did they say this thing or that, or why aren't they saying anything at all? You and I both know there is a world of meaning beneath the words that others say or don't say to us."

"Yes, I'd agree with that," Michael said.

"And yet we don't typically read the scriptures that way," Albert continued. "We read only the words and see only the outward messages. We don't listen to the silence, to the inflection, to the word choice, and so on. We don't ask the question that consumes us during most of our daily lives. We don't ask *Why?* So let's ask that question about the verse we started with." Pointing at the book, he said, "Why do you suppose Nephi bothered to write 'And my father dwelt in a tent'? He easily could have left that line out. Why didn't he? Why did he bother to share that with us?"

Michael remained hesitant.

"Put it together with what we've been pondering in the first verse of the book," Albert prompted.

"You mean the idea that Lehi was wealthy?" Michael asked.

Albert nodded. "So we encounter this wealthy man; a fact that is reinforced in a number of ways as the story continues, by the way." He reached for the Book of Mormon Michael had set on the table between them and turned to the fourth verse of the second chapter of 1 Nephi. "For example, here, read verse 4 of chapter 2," he said, extending the book to Michael.

"'And it came to pass,'" Michael began reading, "'that he

departed into the wilderness. And he left his house, and the land of his inheritance, and his gold, and his silver, and his precious things, and took nothing with him, save it were his family, and provisions, and tents, and departed into the wilderness.'"[5]

"Why did Nephi say it that way?" Albert asked. "He didn't have to list the categories of riches Lehi left, but he did. He left 'his house, *and* the land of his inheritance, *and* his gold, *and* his silver, *and* his precious things.' Why all the *ands?*" Albert asked. "What's the effect of him separately mentioning the various kinds of precious things that Lehi left behind?"

"It really punches up and emphasizes the extent of his wealth," Michael answered.

"Yes," Albert agreed. "And let's look at a verse in chapter 3 as well—verse 16—where Nephi makes another reference to the family's wealth. Go ahead," Albert prodded. "Read it."

Michael turned the page and began reading. "'Wherefore, let us be faithful in keeping the commandments of the Lord; therefore let us go down to the land of our father's inheritance, for behold he left gold and silver, and all manner of riches. And all this he hath done because of the commandments of the Lord.'"[6]

Michael looked up at Albert. "All manner of riches," he repeated.

"Yes," Albert nodded. "It kind of gives you a sense for why Laman and Lemuel didn't want to leave, doesn't it? They were living the life. These weren't common folk who might have left behind a few belongings. They were among the very rich. They had much more to lose than most people. And much more to long for and miss."

Michael nodded contemplatively.

"Which brings us back to the question of *why*," Albert continued. "Nephi didn't have to start his writing with a mention of their wealth. Nor did he need to continue emphasizing it. But he did. He didn't need to say, 'and he left his house, and the land of his inheritance, and his gold, and his silver, and his precious things.' He could have just written that they left their belongings and set off into the wilderness. But he didn't; he emphasized their wealth and how much they had left behind. And he didn't need to share his words to his brothers about how they had 'left gold and silver, and all manner of riches.' He could have just said that he suggested they go and get some of their belongings and try to trade them to Laban for the plates of brass. But he didn't. He again chose to emphasize how much they had left behind. My question for you is, why?"

"I guess it was important to Nephi that we understand how much they were willing to sacrifice."

"But why?" Albert asked again. "So they left a lot behind. So what? Why emphasize it? Why start the book that way? And why repeat the theme? Why?"

"I don't know," Michael shook his head. "Maybe he just wanted us to know that they were willing to leave everything to follow the Lord."

"No matter the cost?" Albert asked. "No matter how great or difficult?"

"Yes."

Albert looked at him. "Okay, then, let's return to the verse we started with. Why do you suppose Nephi bothered to write that his father dwelt in a tent—something he wrote three other times in the book of First Nephi, by the way? Why spend the energy and take the space to write that once, much less four times?"

Michael started nodding to himself. "I see. It's about the stark contrast, isn't it? It's another way of reminding us that Lehi left everything behind—the land of his inheritance, his silver, his gold, all manner of riches, and all of his precious things—that he was willing to sacrifice everything to do what the Lord instructed him to do, and that he was willing to do this no matter the cost, as you said."

"A plausible reading," Albert nodded, "and a reading that comes to the fore only if you wonder *why* as you read: *Why this word, why this verse, why this beginning, why this order,* and so on."

"I'll take you up on that, then," Michael said. "Why this message? Why was it so important to Nephi to emphasize how much they were willing to leave behind? Of all the messages he could have chosen to communicate to the reader, why that one?"

"Ah, an excellent question," Albert smiled. "In answer to it, may I suggest an additional question?"

"How about a good, crisp answer?" Michael joked.

Albert smiled. "You're the lawyer, Michael. If you want an answer from a witness, what do you need to do?"

"Ask him a question," Michael answered. "But you're not answering any of mine, I'm afraid."

"Perhaps not," Albert responded. "But then again, I am not your witness, am I? That would be Nephi. And Moses, and Isaiah, and Matthew, and Paul. Your questions are for the scriptures. Who am I to step in and speak for them?"

Michael didn't say anything.

"So," Albert continued, "another question, then."

6

LOOK FOR PATTERNS

You asked why Nephi apparently chose to emphasize this message of their leaving everything behind."

Michael nodded.

"When looking at a scriptural verse or passage or story, I find it helpful to look for patterns."

"What kind of patterns?"

"Word patterns," Albert responded, "thematic patterns, structural patterns, similitudes, parallelisms, and so on. I try to see if the story resembles other stories or if the theme contains echoes of themes from other places. And I look for interesting patterns within the story itself—interesting repetitions, for example, or comparisons, or juxtapositions. For example, let's take the story we're considering. We have a man who has left everything behind and begun a trek into the wilderness. Can you think of any other scriptural stories that have the same pattern?"

"Sure," Michael answered. "Adam and Eve to begin with."

"Talk more about that," Albert invited.

"Well, they were in the Garden of Eden—a place of perfect plenty. But they had to leave and journey into the wilderness. In their case, they even had to leave the presence of the Lord."

"Okay, excellent," Albert said. "Where else do you see this pattern?"

Michael thought about it. "Noah," he answered. "And Abraham, who left his homeland in the Ur of Chaldeas to go to Canaan. Moses, for that matter, too." He thought about it for another moment. "The ancient apostles too," he said. "They left their livelihoods and followed the Lord.

"And the pioneers as well," he added. "They left everything behind to gather with the Saints." This thought took him to memories of his mission, and to a college-age Japanese man named Yushio Ikeda who had been disowned by his parents and written out of his inheritance as a result of joining the Church. "Most of the people who joined the Church during my mission in Japan had the same kind of experience," he said. "Many of them lost a lot by joining. But they joined anyway."

"Interesting, isn't it?" Albert replied. "This little verse—'and my father dwelt in a tent'—reaches all the way to the densely populated modern cities of Japan. All who listen to the Lord have to give up something and leave things behind. Specifically,

anything that is of the world has to go. Sell all that thou
hast, . . . and come, follow me,'[7] the Lord said to the rich young
man who was wondering what he must do to inherit eternal
life. The rich young man was simply confronting the question
Lehi confronted, and Adam, and Noah, and Moses, and the
apostles, and the pioneers, and the people you taught in Japan
as well. Would he, as Lehi, be willing to leave everything
behind to follow the Lord? He was hardly the first to have to
make that decision. Nor the last. It is one of the most repeated
patterns in the scriptures.

"In fact," he continued, "we haven't yet talked about the
most central place we see this pattern."

"The most central?"

"Yes. But we'll get to it, don't worry."

"With another question, no doubt," Michael said.

"No doubt," Albert smiled. "But let's first go back to the
first chapter of 1 Nephi. It was a pattern in that chapter that
first awakened me to the power of seeing scriptural patterns."

"How were you able to see it?" Michael asked.

"Someone taught me to ask questions."

"Who?"

"Elder Holland."

"Of the Quorum of the Twelve?"

"Yes."

"You know him?"

"No. But I once read something he wrote that helped me

to get curious about the scriptures—something he wrote about 1 Nephi, chapter 1, long before he was called to the Apostleship.[8] Turn to that chapter and I'll show you."

Michael quickly turned the pages. "Okay, I'm ready."

Albert came over and sat down next to Michael on the sofa. Together they looked at the book.

"Look here at verse 4," Albert said, pointing to the verse. "Many prophets began prophesying to the people that Jerusalem would be destroyed unless they repented. Do you see that?"

Michael nodded.

"Was Lehi one of those prophets?" Albert asked.

"I think so," Michael answered.

"Let's take a closer look. Go ahead and read verse 5."

Michael cleared his throat and began reading:

"'Wherefore,'" Michael began, "'it came to pass that my father, Lehi, as he went forth prayed unto the Lord, yea, even with all his heart, in behalf of his people.'"

"What do you suppose it means that he 'went forth'?" Albert asked.

Michael puzzled over that. "It sounds like it might mean that he went out somewhere."

"Out from where?"

Michael looked at the prior verse. "Maybe out from Jerusalem," he said. "That's the location that's mentioned in verse 4."

"Okay," Albert said, "so it sounds like Lehi maybe went out from Jerusalem to pray. Why?"

Michael looked down at what he had just read.

"Look before the *Wherefore*," Albert directed him.

"Because of what the prophets had been saying," Michael replied. "They were saying that the city would be destroyed unless the people repented, so he was praying for the people— in their behalf, it says here in verse 5."

"And what do you suppose he was asking the Lord on their behalf?"

"That they would repent?" Michael wondered aloud.

"Could be," Albert said. "Any other possibilities?"

Michael scanned the verses again. "Or maybe he was asking the Lord to save them."

Albert smiled and took a folded sheet of paper out of his shirt pocket. "I want to jot down what we have discovered so far." He wrote the following:

> 1. **A man was pricked by the words of a prophet.**
> 2. **He went out apart to pray.**

"Okay, let's continue then," he said. "Look at verses 6 and 7. What happened?"

Michael read the verses. "Lehi saw a vision. It reads a little like Moses' experience with the burning bush. Lehi saw a pillar of fire on a rock, and it says that he 'saw and heard much.'"

"Okay, good," Albert said. "So then what happened?"

"It says that what he saw and heard made him 'quake and tremble exceedingly.'"

"Why?" Albert asked.

"Good question. I'm wondering the same thing."

"Let's read verse 7 again, shall we?" Albert said, pulling the book to where he could read it. "'And it came to pass that he returned to his own house at Jerusalem; and he cast himself upon his bed, being overcome with the Spirit and the things which he had seen.'"

Albert looked at Michael. "It sounds like you were right about how he went out from Jerusalem to pray, because here we learn that he afterward returned to his home at Jerusalem. By the way, the word *at* sounds a little strange to the ear, doesn't it? Would you say that you returned to your home *at* Stamford or to your home *in* Stamford?"

"*In* Stamford," Michael answered promptly.

"Me too," Albert agreed. "So you might ask yourself why Nephi is using the word *at* instead of *in,* and whether that might be revealing in some way."

Michael nodded with interest.

"But that's a question for another day," Albert said. "Notice what it says about Lehi's reaction after the vision: he 'cast himself upon his bed.' What does that make it sound like he was feeling?"

"He might just have been tired. But the word *cast* makes it almost sound like he was feeling downtrodden or depressed."

"It does, doesn't it. And why might he have been feeling that way?"

"Maybe he didn't like the answer to his prayer," Michael responded. "He was overcome, it says, by the things that he had seen in the vision."

"Things that had made him 'quake and tremble exceedingly,'" Albert followed up.

"Yes."

"So let's see what happened next. Look at verses 8 and 9."

"He saw another vision," Michael said, after reading. "He saw the Father and the Son."

"Yes," Albert said, adding that as item three on his list. "In verse 9 he says that he saw One descending out of heaven, which in context is clearly a reference to the Savior. The prior verse, verse 8, records that Lehi '*thought* he saw God sitting upon his throne, surrounded with numberless concourses of angels.' One might wonder what is meant by *thought he saw* in the case of the Father and *saw* in the case of the Son. But it seems accurate to say that he saw a vision of the Father and the Son. Now read verse 9 again, along with verses 10 through 12."

Michael read the verses aloud.

> And it came to pass that he saw One descending out of the midst of heaven, and he beheld that his luster was above that of the sun at noon-day. And he also saw twelve others following him, and their brightness did exceed that of the stars in the firmament. And they

came down and went forth upon the face of the earth; and the first came and stood before my father, and gave unto him a book, and bade him that he should read. And it came to pass that as he read, he was filled with the Spirit of the Lord.[9]

"So what did Lehi receive?" Albert asked.

"A book."

Albert nodded and added that to his list. "Now look at verses 15 and 18."

Michael read again.

And after this manner was the language of my father in the praising of his God; for his soul did rejoice, and his whole heart was filled, because of the things which he had seen, yea, which the Lord had shown unto him. . . . Therefore, I would that ye should know, that after the Lord had shown so many marvelous things unto my father, Lehi, yea, concerning the destruction of Jerusalem, behold he went forth among the people, and began to prophesy and to declare unto them concerning the things which he had both seen and heard.[10]

"So had Lehi been among the prophets before this time?" Albert asked.

Michael looked back at the verses. "It doesn't sound like

it," he said. "It says here in verse 18 that after reading the book he *began* to prophesy to the people."

"So he began to preach to the people what he had read in the book," Albert summarized.

"Yes, it seems that way."

Albert again added to his list. "Okay, then, go ahead and read verses 19 and 20."

Michael did so silently and then said, "So after he began to preach to them the things that had been manifest to him and the things that he had read from the book, the people mocked him and sought to kill him."

"Yes," Albert agreed, adding to what he was writing. "So look at the story we encounter in the first chapter of 1 Nephi:

> 1. A man was pricked by the words of a prophet.
> 2. He went out apart to pray.
> 3. He saw a vision of the Father and the Son.
> 4. He received a book.
> 5. He began to preach to the people what he read in the book.
> 6. The people mocked and sought to kill him.

Lehi

"Whose story is that?" Albert asked.

Michael looked at the list to verify what he was thinking. "It's the story of Joseph Smith, isn't it?" he asked in wonder. "It's the story of the Restoration."

"Yes, Michael, it is remarkably similar, isn't it? The restored scriptural work of the Restoration begins with a story that is itself in similitude of the Restoration!" Albert paused to let that settle. "And within that story we encounter a book that, when read, fills the reader with the Spirit of the Lord.[11] What might that imply about the Book of Mormon itself?"

"Are you saying that that implies a promise regarding the Book of Mormon as well—that those who read *it* will be filled with the Spirit of the Lord just as Lehi was?"

"I think the story can be read to imply that, yes," Albert answered. "That is, if one feasts[12] on the Book of Mormon the way Lehi devoured the book he was given to read."

Michael pondered that. As he did so, Albert studied him. "How old are your children, Michael?"

This question pulled Michael from his thoughts. "Hayden is four and Erika is two."

Albert nodded wistfully. Michael remembered that he had seen no pictures of children in the room and wondered if Albert and his wife had been childless. "Think about how children learn to speak," Albert said. "They hear words spoken by the adults around them, but these words are mere sounds that lack intelligible meaning until the child starts to notice patterns and associations. He begins to make the connection that when his mother makes the sound *milk* she hands him a bottle with yummy white liquid in it. And so he makes the connection between the sound *milk* and perhaps the bottle or maybe the liquid. It isn't until he notices this pattern in his mother's speech that he begins to obtain what we might call an under-standing.

"This is true of all learning. We gain understanding only to the degree we come to see connections and recognize patterns. The weatherman who looks at the weather maps, for example, can interpret them with meaning only because he has been trained to see patterns.

"It's the same with the scriptures. No verse is an island. Every part of the word of God is connected to the other words he has spoken to man. Certain phrases and themes appear again and again. Patterns emerge among stories, and we begin to see messages that are conveyed not only through the words on the surface of a passage or chapter, but also in the depth beneath the story—in the common story line, for example, as we see in the Lehi and Joseph Smith stories."

Albert paused. "There is one pattern, however, that is most central of all—a pattern you will begin to see everywhere in the scriptures once you begin looking for it."

This piqued Michael's interest. "What is it?"

Albert smiled. "A pattern that must be discovered to be appreciated."

7

PONDER THE SAVIOR

That's it?" Michael said in exasperation. "You're not going to tell me anything more than that?"

Albert smiled, stood up, and walked to the far bookcase. He removed a leather-bound binder and returned to his seat.

"What's that?" Michael asked.

"A little something I've written," Albert said.

"Really? About what?"

"Your favorite topic," Albert smiled. "The Old Testament."

"You've written a book about the Old Testament?" Michael blurted, duly impressed.

"Well, calling it a book is perhaps too generous. It's something I've mostly written just to myself, so that I won't forget the amazing things I've learned from that work of scripture."

Michael was interested. "Like what?"

"Like the central pattern I just mentioned," Albert replied, as he searched the pages of his writing for something. "Yes, here we are," he said. "I'd like to give you a little quiz, if you don't mind. Are you game?"

Michael didn't feel confident in his knowledge of the Old Testament, but he knew how to take a test. "Sure."

"Okay, then," Albert said, sizing Michael up from over the top of his glasses, "I'm going to describe some characters from the Old Testament. Your job is to tell me who I'm describing."

"Okay."

"Here is the first. He was the firstborn and created in the image of God."

Michael immediately thought of Adam.

Continuing, Albert said, "He chose to leave the presence of God to fulfill the plan of salvation and then chose to partake of bitterness in a garden. He took upon himself death so that all might live. He was the person through whom the gospel was delivered to all mankind and was set up to be at the head of mankind. He reigns as our father forever."

Albert looked up at Michael. "Who is that?" he asked.

"I think it's Adam," Michael answered.

"And who else?" Albert asked.

"Who else?"

"Yes. Who else chose to partake of bitterness in a garden? Who else took upon himself death so that all might live? Who else reigns as our father forever?"

"Christ?"

Albert smiled. "Very good, Michael. That is both the story of Adam and the story of Christ.

"Here's another: This man was the chosen son. The scriptures describe him as 'perfect.' His likeness was the express likeness of his father. And he was like unto his father in all things."

"Christ?"

"Yes. And who else?" Albert asked.

Michael searched his mind for an answer. "I'm not sure."

"That is Seth," Albert said. "And Christ as well."

"Here's another: This man preached tirelessly to a people who largely rejected him. He was just and perfect in his generation. But he was mocked by the people. Grieved by their sins, he did all that the Lord commanded him. The people sought to kill him. He constructed the means of saving all mankind. Those who followed him were saved from death. Only those who were his family were saved. His salvation also saved the animals from death."

The last one gave it away. "That's Noah," Michael said.

"Yes. And who else?"

"Christ," he whispered as he replayed the elements in his mind.

"How about this one," Albert said. "He was a great high priest. None was greater. He offered the Lord's Supper. He established righteousness among his followers and was known as the 'prince of peace,' the 'king of heaven,' and the 'king of peace.' The Holy Priesthood was named after him."

Albert looked at Michael again. "Who's that?"

"Melchizedek?"

"And—"

"And Christ," Michael answered.

"You're seeing the pattern?"

"All of these Old Testament individuals are in similitude of Christ."

"Yes, and we've only just begun," Albert said. "A few more for you and then we'll quit: There was a long wait for this person's birth. His name and birth were foretold by an angel. His mother conceived miraculously and brought forth a son. He was called 'the only begotten son.' He traveled to Jerusalem on a donkey. Those with him were asked to wait while he went yonder to worship and pray. He was to be sacrificed on a hill in the area of Moriah. He carried the wood to be instrumental in his death. He was one with, and in similitude of, his father. He voluntarily submitted to the will of his father. Those who accept the gospel become his seed—his sons and his daughters."

"That's Isaac," Michael said.

Albert looked at him.

"And Christ as well," Michael added.

"How about this one: He was the beloved son. He declared that he would be the ruler over the children of Israel, who saw him as taking authority over them and rejected and hated him.

He sought out his brethren on behalf of his father, but the children of Israel conspired to kill him. Judah—which in Greek is Judas—betrayed him to the gentiles. He was sold for the price of a slave of his age, in pieces of silver. The attempt to destroy him set in motion events that saved the children of Israel from death. He was taken captive and placed under the dominion of an officer of the strongest army of the world. He resisted temptation perfectly but was falsely accused. He began his ministry of preparing salvation for Israel when he was thirty years old. He provided bread and water to Israel and saved them from death. He offered that bread without price. He provided as well the opportunity for sinners to repent and forgave those who had caused him to suffer. He was recognized and accepted by his people only the second time they met. All bowed to him."

Michael was stunned by the extent of the parallelism. "Joseph and Christ," he whispered, his mind racing.

"One more for now: This person's birth and mission as a deliverer of Israel was prophesied. The king at the time of his birth commanded that the children of his age be put to death. His parents saved him from death by sending him into Egypt. He spent forty days fasting and communing with God before taking the gospel to Israel. He was rejected when he first went to Israel. He resisted and rebuked Satan, performed many miracles, and had power over the elements. He preferred not to have to do what he was to do, but he submitted to the will of

God. He fed his followers with bread from heaven and brought a new law. He delivered Israel from bondage. He was the mediator of the covenant between God and man." Albert looked at Michael. "Who's that?"

"Moses," Michael whispered. "And Christ."

"And that's only the beginning," Albert said. "The lives of most Old Testament characters you've heard of, and many you have not, are in similitude of Christ—Adam, Seth, Noah, Melchizedek, Abraham, Isaac, Jacob, Joseph, Gideon, Jephthah, Samson, Samuel, David, Abigail, Elijah, Job, Jonah, Isaiah, Maher-shalal-hash-baz, Eliakim, Jeremiah, and Daniel, to name a few. In important ways, the lives of these and other individuals parallel the life of the Savior, each of them illuminating different aspects of his mission."

"Maher-shalal who?" Michael asked. "That's someone in the Old Testament?"

"Sure is," Albert answered. "And like the rest, his story points to Christ's. In fact, here it is." Albert looked back down at his writings and read the following. "His birth and name were foretold. Directly after it was prophesied that a son would be born of a virgin, his mother conceived and brought forth a son. He was named according to the prophecy. His birth was a sign that the land of Israel would soon be forsaken and that the Israelites would be scattered from the land."

"I've never heard of him," Michael said, shaking his head.

"He doesn't get much attention," Albert remarked, "so

that's not surprising. But what is surprising is the extent of Christ's mission that is revealed through the parallel lives of many of the scriptural characters who preceded him. I did a little experiment. I charted these parallelisms by character, even such characters as the personification of Wisdom in Proverbs and the House of Israel itself, both of which parallel Christ. I then put those various parallelisms together to see how much of Christ's life and mission were foretold through them."

"And?" Michael asked after a moment's pause.

"I was dumbfounded by the extent of the Christ-centered prophecies that lay hidden in the patterns of these characters' lives. Utterly amazed and dumbfounded. This is why the apostle Paul said, 'until this day remaineth the same vail untaken away in the reading of the old testament; which vail is done away in Christ.'[13] His entire mission is laid out in the Old Testament."

Michael's interest was piqued. "Could you share some of it with me?" he asked.

Albert looked at him thoughtfully. "Perhaps," he said. "But not yet."

Michael's shoulders slumped a bit.

"In due time, Michael," Albert said. "We're only just getting started here. We haven't even asked the next question we need to ask about the verse we've been pondering."

"What question is that?" Michael asked.

"Let's first review what we've done so far," Albert said. "We began by asking *What?*—what's the context, what's the meaning of this or that word, and so on. Then we wondered *Why*—why this word and not another, for example, why this order, why this tone? Then we began looking for *patterns*—word patterns, linguistic structures, repetitions, thematic echoes, parallelisms, and the like. Which brings us to the next question: *What does this verse, story, or passage reveal about Christ and the Atonement?*"

Albert paused for a moment. "So what *does* it reveal about Christ and the Atonement?" he asked.

"What does *what* reveal?" Michael asked.

"'And my father dwelt in a tent,'" Albert answered. "What does that verse have to do with Christ?"

Michael thought back on their conversation. *Lehi left everything behind—his riches, his status, his comfort. Just as Christ did,* Michael realized. *He condescended from heaven to the realm of fallen man. He left everything behind.* "Christ left everything behind too," he said.

"Yes, he certainly did. And what is it that he left behind?"

"Power," Michael answered. "Godhood, perfection."

"Anything else?"

Michael thought about it. Nothing more came to mind.

"What about in the Garden of Gethsemane? What did he leave behind there?"

"The safety and peace of his sinlessness," Michael answered, his mind suddenly racing again. "He didn't deserve to suffer for sins, but he did. He could have returned to the Father on his own merits, sinless as he was. But he didn't."

"No, he didn't," Albert agreed. "Like Adam in the Garden of Eden, the Savior in the Garden of Gethsemane decided not to be a lone man in paradise, but rather chose to partake of bitterness so that man may live—eternally."

Michael was awestruck. "He actually left everything, didn't he?" he said. "His freedom from pain and suffering for sin, for example. He left it all."

"Yes. Another way to say it is that he took upon himself everything we have failed to leave behind. All of our sins and weaknesses, for example, the grudges we carry, our quickness to anger. He took upon himself everything that has become too precious to us—everything we are refusing to give up—in order to provide a way that we can be relieved of those burdens. Metaphorically speaking, he could have stayed, as Laman and Lemuel longed to stay, in Jerusalem. But he didn't. He left everything behind by taking upon himself what we must leave behind but haven't. That was his wilderness—the stark reality of our sins and suffering."

Michael didn't know what to say, and the two of them sat in silence for a few moments.

"Which brings us," Albert said, "to a fifth question I ask when I'm studying the scriptures."

8

APPLY TO ONESELF

After I have asked *what* and wondered *why,* after I have looked for patterns and pondered the Savior, then—with what I have learned in mind—I apply the verse or passage or story to myself. When I read, my final question is: <u>How is this story about me?"</u>

Albert paused and looked at Michael. "So how *is* this story about you, Michael?" he asked. "What haven't you been willing to leave behind?" He tilted his head down and looked over the top of his glasses. "Anger perhaps? A grudge or two? Or maybe a habit or tendency that offends the Spirit."

Michael's mind took him to three days earlier. He was rushing to get Angie and the kids out the door and to the airport for their trip to Seattle. Angie was running behind, as usual, and was getting after Michael for not doing enough to help. Michael took offense. "*Listen, Angie,*" he bellowed, "*I've been working just as hard as you have here. I did breakfast, got the kids bathed, and even dressed them. If we're running late, maybe you're the problem.*"

"I might get angry sometimes," Michael allowed. "But who doesn't?"

Albert continued peering at him from above the rims of his glasses. Michael looked away, feeling uncomfortable under the gaze.

"And grudges?" Albert followed up.

Michael looked at the ground and thought of his father. They'd never been very close. His dad was an alcoholic who cared so little about Michael that he scarcely noticed when Michael left the family's Catholicism to join a new faith. Never even mentioned it. On his mission, Michael wrote him regularly, openly sharing his experiences in hopes that his father would become interested in the gospel. But the interest never came.

At that very moment his father was lying in a hospital bed, ravaged by diabetes brought on by a lifetime of bad habits. In the last year and a half, he had gone from being slowed down by diabetes to gradually being killed by it. First, he lost a foot due to infection. Then both his legs above the knee. His brain function was now very slow, his kidneys near complete failure, and he had lost his will to survive. The family had recently made the decision to put him on hospice care.

As Michael sat thinking about it, and in light of Albert's question, he realized he wouldn't even be sad when his father died. *So do I carry a grudge toward my father?* he asked himself. *I suppose I do.* To which he added internally, *Who wouldn't?*

"You see," Albert said, interrupting Michael's thoughts, "anger and grudges rob us of the Spirit and keep us from the Lord. 'First be reconciled to thy brother,' Christ said, after teaching that whoever is angry with his brother shall be in danger of the judgment, 'and then come unto me with full purpose of heart, and I will receive you.' Until we can leave our anger and bitterness behind, we're at risk of perishing with Jerusalem.

"The same is true of habits that offend the Spirit," Albert continued. "Or perhaps you have become too attached to certain things—to activities or pursuits that have become too precious. More precious, even, than what is holy."

Things that are holy—Michael's mind went to the temple. He hadn't been in months. He told himself he didn't have the time. But he knew that wasn't true. He'd managed to golf a fair amount over the same period. He heard Albert's words again: *Perhaps you have become too attached to activities or pursuits that have become too precious. More precious, even, than what is holy.*

His shoulders slumped. That was certainly true as far as the temple was concerned. *But is that my fault?* he countered within. He wondered if the Church shouldn't update the temple experience to make it more relevant to the modern day. This thought emboldened him. He had come to Albert to learn about loving holiness. That meant loving the temple too. But what if the antipathy he was currently feeling wasn't entirely his fault? This idea gave him the cover he needed. "There *is* one thing I know I should be enjoying that I'm really not," he said.

"And what is that?" Albert asked.

"Going to the temple," Michael answered.

Albert laid his binder down on the coffee table and leaned back in his chair.

"You don't like the temple," he said, looking at Michael.

"Not really, no."

"What is it you don't like about it?"

"I find it incredibly boring," Michael replied. And then he added, "Don't you?"

Albert shook his head. "There was a time when I thought that. But not anymore. Now there's no place I'd rather be."

Michael had heard others say this before, but it seemed incredible to him. He wasn't sure he believed them—or Albert in this moment.

"How can that be?" Michael asked. "How can you go from thinking something is entirely boring to preferring it to every-thing else?"

"I used to think the scriptures were boring too," Albert answered. "But have you been bored by the conversation we've had around 1 Nephi 2:15?"

Michael had become so caught up in the dialogue that he had almost forgotten about the verse that started it. He and

Albert had asked what, wondered why, looked for patterns, pondered the Savior, and finally applied the scripture to themselves. He thought of the recurring theme of leaving everything behind, and how he himself, like Laman and Lemuel, might be clutching to the remnants of Jerusalem, unwilling to leave his anger, his grudges, and his worldly preferences behind. This thought caught him up short, as he had never really identified himself with Laman and Lemuel before. But he could see his resemblance to them now, and it worried him.

His mind then turned to the fascinating patterns they had discussed—how Lehi's story, for example, was parallel with Joseph Smith's. And how so many characters in the scriptures are actually in similitude of Christ. Michael had been taken by the entire discussion.

"No," he finally answered. "Our discussion has been really interesting, actually."

"As the temple will become to you," Albert said, "if you understand what it's about—learning about it and attending with the same kind of curiosity we have had around Nephi's father dwelling in a tent."

Michael thought about the teachings in the temple—teachings he had by then witnessed dozens of times. He didn't know if he could muster the level of curiosity Albert had brought to 1 Nephi 2:15.

Noticing the sudden drop in Michael's countenance, Albert said, "Are you willing to attempt curiosity about the temple,

Michael? Are you willing to engage it in conversation, the way we have been engaged with the scriptures?"

How could a person say "No" to that question, even if he wanted to? Michael nodded without enthusiasm.

"Then I have an assignment for you," Albert said.

"Go to the temple?" Michael asked flatly, anticipating the answer.

"If you'd like," Albert said.

The openness of that answer surprised Michael.

"But I *would* like you to do something else," Albert added.

"What?"

"Read."

"Read what?"

"The first five chapters of the book of Mosiah."

"King Benjamin's address?" Michael asked.

Albert nodded.

"But that's not about the temple. Is it?"

Albert smiled. "Yes and no. King Benjamin's address actually happened at the temple. You will find, however, that most who heard it were listening from outside the structure."

Michael frowned. "How is that relevant?"

"It might not be," Albert replied. "But we learn from King Benjamin that there is something we must know before we are equipped to enter, understand, and benefit from the temple."

"What's that?"

"We need to understand that we are ill. Utterly and completely ill."

Michael stared at Albert for a moment in silence. "I'm not sure I know what you mean."

"Then you might be interested in King Benjamin's words, and in what happens to his people."

Michael reached for the book.

"Not now, Michael. We don't have enough time."

"Then when?"

Albert looked at him for a moment. "How long did you say Angela was out of town?"

"Until Saturday."

"Then you'll be alone at home."

Michael nodded.

"Perfect conditions for a conversation."

"But I'd like you to be in on that conversation as well," Michael said, hopefully.

"Very well. If you can feast on King Benjamin's words by tomorrow evening, what do you say we do family home evening together?"

Michael smiled. "Thanks, Albert. I'd like that."

"Good." Nodding toward Michael's empty glass he added, "I'll have more of that lemonade-flavored water waiting for you."

PART II

LOVING THE
HOLY SABBATH

9

UNREST

Despite the late hour, Michael climbed under his covers and opened the Book of Mormon to the first chapter of Mosiah.

Given the discussion he'd had with Albert, he found it interesting that the first seven verses amounted to a sermon about the importance of scripture study. "I would that ye should remember to search [the scriptures] diligently," King Benjamin told his sons, "that ye may profit thereby."[15] Michael set the book down for a moment and looked up at the ceiling. The words *search* and *diligently* brought Albert's five questions to mind: *Ask what, wonder why, look for patterns, ponder the Savior,* and *apply to me.* Mere reading was not enough.

He looked at the book again and reread verse 7. He was struck by the phrase, "that you may profit thereby." The word *that* implied that we won't profit from the scriptures *unless* we search them diligently. Michael's own experience with the scriptures over the years was evidence of this.

Beginning in verse 9, he came to the story he remembered. King Benjamin, now quite old, called his son Mosiah before him and appointed him to be his successor. He gave Mosiah charge over all the sacred writings in his possession, as well as the sacred artifacts that had been handed down from the time of Lehi and Nephi. He then directed Mosiah to gather the people together to the temple at Zarahemla to hear his final words as their king.[16]

As Michael continued reading, he saw things in the story he hadn't noticed before. For example, he was struck by the directional clue in the first verse of chapter 2, where it said that the people went "up" to the temple to hear King Benjamin's words. *Was it in the mountains?* he wondered. *Or was it perhaps on a hill?* The questions brought him a little closer to the story.

Verse 3 revealed that the people brought the firstlings of their flock to the temple to offer sacrifice and burnt offerings according to the law of Moses. *Was it Passover time?* It was a question that had never occurred to Michael. The next verse said the people did this that they "might give thanks to the Lord their God, who had brought them out of the land of Jerusalem, and who had delivered them out of the hands of their enemies."[17] Michael was struck by the parallelism: *These people gathered for sacrifice to the temple to commemorate the*

Lord's deliverance just as the Passover under the law of Moses com-memorates the Lord bringing the Israelites out from their bondage in the land of Egypt.

He continued on.

The people arranged themselves by families into tents, with the doors of the tents toward the temple so that they could hear the words of King Benjamin.[18] *Why tents?* he wondered. It occurred to him that this gathering might have lasted for some time. *But why would they LISTEN to him from inside their tents?* he asked. *Perhaps it frequently rained,* he reasoned, imagining the scene. How strange it must have been for King Benjamin to look out over the host of his people and see only a sea of tents! Michael chuckled at the vision.

As he scanned verses 5 and 6 again, he was thunderstruck by a connection he had never made until that moment: The people were gathered into their homes, as it were, by family—in fact, the verse emphasized that "every family [was] separate one from another"—with the doors of their tents or homes oriented toward the temple. *Our families need to be oriented to the temple!* He looked up at the ceiling and sighed. Although his mind was captured by the insight, his heart lagged behind. His faith system told him he should be taking the temple more seriously than he was, but try as he might, he couldn't conjure enough interest to overcome the indifference that had accumulated within him over the years.

He resumed reading.

Verses 7 and 8 made it seem like King Benjamin might have been surprised by the number of people who had gathered, as verse 7 said that because of the greatness of the multitude, he caused that a tower be built for him to speak from, so that he could speak to the people who were outside the temple as well as those who were within. *Oh, that's what Albert was referring to when he said that most who listened to the king did so from outside the temple,* he thought.

Although Michael was unconscious of it, every question brought the story a little more to life for him. He was by now picturing the temple, its setting, the throng of tents, and the families that filled them. In his mind's eye he could see the wooden tower rising above the temple wall, and he imagined a covering over its top that would protect the king from the elements. For whatever reason, he pictured as well a grand range of lushly covered mountains in the distance beyond.

He then imagined two men, one aged and being helped by the other, slowly ascending a wide ladder to the platform on the top of the tower. As the men pulled themselves up, a hush fell over the multitude. The aged one stepped haltingly forward, his eggshell-colored robe and brilliant white hair blowing in the breeze.

He stretched his trembling arms toward the people beyond the front of the temple. Then, looking from side to side, he slowly reached outward to the multitudes on either side. "My brethren," he cried in a powerful voice that belied his condition and years, "I have not commanded you to come up hither to trifle with the words which I shall speak, but that you should hearken unto me, and open your ears that ye may hear, and your hearts that ye may understand, and your minds that the mysteries of God may be unfolded to your view."[19]

The boldness of the words made Michael shudder. He readied himself for the direct and frank message to come.

But he had forgotten what came next. Instead of railing on them, King Benjamin told them that he was no better than they were, that his aim had simply been to serve them, and that he, like they, were unprofitable servants before the Lord, eternally indebted to the Lord forever and ever.[20] "Therefore," he said, "of what have ye to boast? . . . Can ye say aught of yourselves?" he followed up. "I answer you, Nay. Ye cannot say that ye are even as much as the dust of the earth. . . . And I, even I, whom ye call your king, am no better than ye yourselves are. . . .

"But, O my people," he continued, "beware lest there shall arise contentions among you, and ye list to obey the evil spirit. . . . For behold, there is a wo pronounced upon him who listeth to obey that spirit; for if he listeth to obey him, and remaineth . . . in his sins, the same drinketh damnation to his own soul; for he receiveth for his wages an everlasting punishment."[21]

Michael put the book down. He squinted until the clouds he had imagined overhead had dissipated and he lay staring at his ceiling. *Contention.* The word, and King Benjamin's warning about it, troubled Michael. At that very moment, his father was in hospice care on a bed in Michael's sister's home in Hackensack, New Jersey. His father might die any day, but Michael had no interest in seeing him.

At Angie's insistence, she and Michael had visited him the day before she left for Seattle. They were about to leave that day when his father struggled to lift his arm and hold out his hand to Michael. With the ventilation tube in his throat he couldn't speak. Seeing the pleading look in his father's eyes, Michael reluctantly took the hand. A look of relief then came over his father's face and his father weakly squeezed Michael's hand. It was all the strength he could gather.

To Michael it was much too little and far too late. One needy handclasp couldn't make up for what he felt was a lifetime of irresponsible neglect. Michael slipped his hand away and walked out the door.

"He's your father, Michael!" Angie had yelled at him as they drove away.

"Is that what you call him?" Michael had shouted back. "Is that why you yourself made a point of not bringing the kids—because he's such a loving father and grandfather? Is that why you were so happy to leave them home?"

"That's not fair, Michael."

"I'll tell you what's not fair," he had responded. "It's not fair that I was raised by an alcoholic bum. That's what's not fair!"

"Honestly, Michael, it's as if you're the one who is dying or something. Can't you find a shred of mercy?"

"Mercy is all I ever gave him," Michael had lied. "It's the way I explained away his indifference all these years. I'm sorry if I'm in short supply anymore."

Angie just shook her head. "But he's your father," she had whispered.

"Not for long," Michael spat back, his eyes looking ramrod straight up the road.

The steely glare was now gone from his eyes, but as Michael looked ceiling-ward, he still felt the hot embers of contention smoldering within him. King Benjamin's words came to his mind again: *Beware lest . . . ye list to obey the evil spirit, [for] the same drinketh damnation to his own soul.*[22] Michael shook his head to rid himself of the thought.

He resumed reading at verse 38.

Therefore if that man repenteth not, and remaineth and dieth an enemy to God, the demands of divine justice do awaken his immortal soul to a lively sense of his own guilt, which doth cause him to shrink from the presence of the Lord, and doth fill his breast with guilt, and pain, and anguish, which is like an unquenchable fire, whose flame ascendeth up forever and ever.[23]

He snapped the book shut and stared at the ceiling.

After a minute or so, he set the book on his nightstand and turned off the light.

Mind racing, he fought his way toward sleep.

10

A MEEK AND LOWLY TRUTH

H ello, Michael," Albert welcomed. "Please come in."
Michael dragged himself through the door.

Albert patted him affectionately on the back as they walked
into the living room. "How was your day?"

"Long."

Albert stopped and attempted to look into his eyes. "One
of those, huh?"

Michael kept walking toward the couch. "Yeah," he said.

Albert slowly walked over and sat down in the chair opposite him. "What's wrong?"

Michael shook his head. "Nothing to worry about."

"Something at work?" Albert followed up.

"Yeah," Michael lied. Truth was, his internal argument

about his father had kept him up much of the night. He'd arrived at work more than an hour late for a meeting he had forgotten about, and the rest of his day had been a frantic attempt to catch up.

It was one more thing to blame his father about.

"Did you get a chance to study King Benjamin's words?"

Michael stared at the coffee table. "Some of them."

Albert reached for his Book of Mormon. "Where'd you get to?"

Michael shook his head. "I'm not sure of the verse. I think it was in chapter 2. It was something about how those who list to obey the evil spirit drink damnation to their souls, or something uplifting like that."

Albert nodded, studying Michael's face. "That's when he started warning his people not to let contentions arise between them."

Michael nodded sullenly.

"Why did you stop there?" Albert asked.

Without looking up, Michael said, "I got tired."

Albert laid the book on his lap. "Are you sure you want to do this tonight?"

The comment jerked Michael back to the moment, and he looked up. "Yes, absolutely," he said. "Sorry, Al. Just a tough day I guess."

"Then maybe we should talk another time, and you can go get some rest."

Michael waved the idea off. "No, I'm fine. Let's talk."

Albert eyed him for a moment. "Very well. Then what bit of contention would you like to talk about?"

Albert's directness unnerved Michael. "What do you mean?"

"I don't normally get tired when the Lord is telling me I'm on the road to hell," Albert replied.

"He was talking about those who have let contention enter their lives," Michael protested weakly.

"Exactly. And if you are without any contention, you're about the first person I've met who is."

Michael shifted uncomfortably in his seat.

"So what contention in your life didn't you want to think about?" Albert asked.

Michael looked down at his hands. Something about Al made it impossible for him to withhold. "It's my father," he said.

"Your father," Albert repeated. "What about him?"

"He's a bum," Michael blurted before he could stop himself.

"A *bum?*" Albert's eyebrows raised in surprise.

Hearing himself say it, Michael's resolve hardened. "Yes, an alcoholic shell of embarrassing indifference. He's a bum. Soon a dead one, too, due to conditions he himself has caused."

"Where is he?" Albert asked.

"My sister's place in Hackensack. Probably won't survive another week."

"I'm sorry to hear that," Albert said. "What a tragedy."

"He's a tragedy all right."

Albert looked at Michael for a moment without speaking. "Your feelings are bitter."

"Yours would be too if he was your father."

Albert nodded and looked down at his lap. "Maybe so."

"I'd bet against maybe."

Albert looked up at Michael. "How do you feel about *me?*" he asked meekly.

Michael looked at him. "You?"

Albert nodded.

Michael's mood changed instantly. "I think you're amazing, Al." He looked down at his lap. "You're everything I wish my father could have been."

Albert sat in silence for a moment. "I'm afraid there's something you don't know about me, Michael," he finally said. "I hope it doesn't change your opinion."

Michael looked up at him. "Of course not."

"I'm afraid it might."

Michael's head cocked to the side. He wondered what Albert was talking about.

"I was once the very bum you are describing."

"You?" he reacted. "A bum? What are you talking about, Al?"

Albert breathed in deeply. He put his hands on his thighs and pushed himself up. "Well, that's just it; I don't talk about it much. Still trying to hide my sins, I guess." He slowly walked toward the window.

The room started to spin around Michael. "But I thought you went on a mission," he said.

Albert nodded tentatively. "I did."

"And weren't you married in the temple?"

Albert looked over at the pictures of Helen. "Yes, we were."

"Then what are you talking about?"

"Appearances can deceive, I'm afraid." He turned and looked at Michael. "I've had some pretty significant bumps in the road."

"Like what? It couldn't have been that bad."

Albert exhaled sadly and looked down at the floor. "Helen and I had some tough times, Michael. Dark times. It turns out we couldn't have children, and that challenge morphed into other challenges. I became embittered and resentful—at her, at the Lord, at my life. Finally, I couldn't take it anymore, and I left." He looked up. "I left Helen, Michael."

Michael tried to hide his surprise with forced nonchalance. "Okay, well, you got back together."

"Not until after I'd done some shameful things."

Michael didn't know what to say. "How long were you separated?" he finally asked.

"Almost three years." Albert turned and looked out the window again. "That's when I started drinking."

Michael sat in stunned silence.

Albert turned back to him. "I told you I was a bum, Michael. There was a period of time when I even ended up on the street."

Michael shook his head, trying to clear his mind.

"For a time, anyway," Albert continued. "Until I was taken in."

Michael cleared his throat. "By whom?"

"By a great man," Albert answered. "A grocer by the name of Henry Johnson."

"Of Johnson's Market?" Michael asked.

Albert gazed again out the window. "Yes. It's where he graciously gave me a job. Even though I didn't deserve it."

"But you and Helen got back together," he repeated.

Albert nodded. "Yes."

"How?"

Albert didn't respond for a moment. "I'd been off the streets for a few weeks," he began, still gazing out the window. "Henry had set me up in his guest room. His wife, Martha, had fed me well, and the two of them together nursed my spirit. They were a devout Lutheran couple, and we spent the evenings over dinner talking about spiritual things. I told them that I, myself, was a Mormon, but that I was ashamed by how I had so completely failed to live what I believed.

"I remember Henry opening the Bible to the parable of the prodigal son.[24]

"'I know the parable,' I told him. 'I am the prodigal.'

"'Then you are a fortunate man indeed,' he answered.

"'Fortunate!' I bellowed back with a sarcastic laugh. 'I've lost it all—my membership in my church, my marriage. I've lost everything.'

"'Yes,' he responded, 'and how fortunate it is that you have seen that. Not everyone in the parable did.'

"'Who do you mean?' I asked him.

"'The elder son, of course,' he responded. 'He had lost everything too; he just didn't see it.'

"I argued the point. 'The elder son hadn't lost a thing,' I said. 'He stayed at his father's house. He had it all.'

"'On the contrary,' Henry argued back, 'the only son in the parable that we know entered his father's house is the younger one—the prodigal—not the elder son. The elder son stayed without, railing against his father for the injustice he thought he'd received.'"

At the mention of the sons' father, Michael fidgeted uncomfortably.

"Henry explained to me that the elder son was no less of a sinner than the younger one; he just couldn't see it. 'Look at the context,' Henry said. 'The Lord told this parable to a group of Pharisees—the "elder sons" of their era—after they had questioned why he was hanging out with sinners.[25] The audacious statement the Lord put in the elder son's mouth shows that the Lord did not want us to miss the biting irony. He quotes the elder son as saying, "neither transgressed I at any time thy commandment."[26] That, of course, is true of no one, and makes the elder son a sinner as well.'[27]

"'The elder son, like the Pharisees who couldn't understand Jesus' willingness to receive sinners, couldn't get over the fact that his sinful brother had been received with open arms into his father's house, even with gifts that he himself had not been given—a robe, for example, and the finest feast.[28] It didn't seem fair to him; it didn't seem right. And the parable ends without us knowing whether the elder son ever entered in. All that his father possessed awaited him,[29] but we don't know if he allowed himself to enjoy it. The so-called sinner had been admitted into his father's house, while the so-called righteous son had barred himself from entry.'

"After explaining all this, Henry looked at me and said, 'Just as it was for these sons, our reward in the eternities depends on our realizing just how prodigal we are. Only then are we open to the repentance and healing that we need.' Then he repeated, 'So if you are the prodigal, Al, you are fortunate indeed.'"

Albert fell silent.

In the hush that followed, Michael became acutely aware of his heart pounding at the walls of his chest. This was not only a story from the scriptures—or even, for that matter, a narrative from Albert's life. The story had implications for Michael as well. He could feel it. Like heat on a wound. A bead of perspiration trickled down the side of his face. He wiped at it the way one might swat at a fly.

Albert turned from the window and looked at Michael. "Do you remember yesterday when I said that King Benjamin would teach you about an illness we all share—an illness that will destroy us unless we are healed from it?"

Michael nodded. "But I don't remember reading about any illness."

Albert raised his eyebrows and peered at Michael over the tops of his glasses. "You would have had you continued reading beyond chapter 2." His reproving look retreated quickly into a smile.

"Yes, well, there is that," Michael grinned. "Perhaps a symptom of the illness, would you say?"

"Very likely," Albert chuckled. "This illness of spirit goes by various names. I'll introduce what for me is the most helpful way to think about it by stating what the scriptures say is its cure: a new heart.[30] If the cure for our illness is a change of heart, then what would you say is our malady?"

"Our hearts are impure," Michael responded.

"Exactly, which for me yields a memorable way to think about the spiritual illness we each suffer from. You might think about it this way: Replacement of something is necessary when that thing doesn't work as it needs to—that is, when it's *broken.*

If our hearts need to be replaced or changed, then it follows that our hearts are broken; we need new ones. Although I find this way of thinking about it to be powerfully helpful, we normally talk about broken hearts in a slightly different way in the Church, using the expression to communicate a state of meekness rather than a state of deficiency. In order to avoid confusion while at the same time preserving the power of thinking about our insufficiency before the Lord as a profound brokenness, I use the term *broken nature* to identify our fundamental, fallen condition—our unholiness before the Lord.[31] Our natures are broken with respect to spiritual things and need to be changed, replaced, healed.[32] *That,* I would suggest to you, Michael, is our malady.

"Although the Great Physician stands ready to perform this purifying miracle and to change our broken natures," Albert continued, "he can do so only if we return to him for the surgery—that is, only if we become as the repentant prodigal and contritely recognize our brokenness."

"A contrite spirit—" Michael's voice trailed off.

"Yes. As the prophet Alma taught, 'none but the truly penitent are saved.'[33] The younger and elder sons in the parable were each broken, but only one of them was contrite, and therefore only one of them walked over the threshold into their father's house."

Albert turned again to look out the window, and Michael again became aware of the beating in his chest. His pulse was quickening.

"So, Michael," he said, turning back to face him, "which son are you?"

11

A MIGHTY NEED

Michael could feel the blood rushing to his face. He cleared his throat. "Which son am I?"

"Yes."

Michael thought of the way he congratulated himself for his relative righteousness when compared to his father. The same logic, however, would seem to require him to elevate himself over Albert, something he couldn't begin to do. "Maybe the elder one," he allowed.

"Then you're in a predicament."

"I suppose so."

"If you only *suppose,* then you don't really know." Albert reached for the scriptures. "Let me read you something."

> Behold, it is my will, that all they who call on my name, and worship me according to mine everlasting

gospel, should gather together, and stand in holy places; and prepare for the revelation which is to come, when the veil of the covering of my temple, in my tabernacle, which hideth the earth, shall be taken off, and all flesh shall see me together. And every corruptible thing, both of man, or of the beasts of the field, or of the fowls of the heavens, or of the fish of the sea, that dwells upon all the face of the earth, shall be consumed.[34]

"What's a corruptible thing?" Michael asked.

"A very important question," Albert nodded, "for all that is corruptible will be unable to abide the presence of the Lord in his glory. All that is corruptible will be consumed."

"So what is corruptible?" Michael repeated.

Albert turned a few pages back in the scriptures. Extending the book to Michael and pointing at a particular verse, he said, "Go ahead and read this verse."

Michael took the book and began reading.

> Verily, verily, I say unto you, darkness covereth the earth, and gross darkness the minds of the people, and all flesh has become corrupt before my face.[35]

"So you tell me, Michael," Albert said. "What is corruptible?"

Michael reread the verse and then in hushed voice replied, "It says that we are."

"Yes. That is our predicament. Since the fall of Adam, mankind has been separated from God, a separation known as spiritual death.[36] The predicament of spiritual death is captured by the Lord's statement to Moses about the fate of corruptible man: 'No sinful man hath at any time,' he said, 'neither shall there be any sinful man at any time, that shall see my face and live.'[37] Elsewhere he said, 'He who is not able to abide the law of a celestial kingdom *cannot* abide a celestial glory,' for 'no unclean thing *can* dwell there, or dwell in his presence.'[38] In these and other passages, the Lord is not merely saying that no unclean thing will be *allowed* to dwell in his presence. He is actually making an even stronger point: he is saying that no unclean thing will be *able* to dwell with him. We cannot be with God unless and until we are sanctified and made holy like he is. Which means, Michael, that all that is ungodly within us must be put to death or we will not be able to enter his presence."

The words echoed within Michael, *All that is ungodly within us must be put to death or we will not be able to enter God's presence.* He winced under the weight of the thought.

"This, then," Albert continued, "is the predicament of man—my predicament and yours: Having become sinful, our natures having become broken, we cannot abide the glory of sinlessness. When the Lord comes in glory, who will be able to endure it? As Malachi famously put it, given that all that is corruptible will be consumed by 'the brightness of his coming,' 'who may abide the day of his coming? and who shall stand when he appeareth?'[39] Even more, when we are called to stand before the fullness of the glory of the Father, who will be able to abide *that* day?"

Michael waited for an answer. "So who *can* endure it?" he asked.

"Only those who are sanctified and made holy, changed into beings who can abide the glory of God."

"So how does that happen?" Michael asked.

"You mean how does the Lord have power to change us? Or do you mean what do we have to do in order to *allow* him to change us?"

Michael thought about it. "Both, I suppose."

"As one who has been painfully aware of his own need to change, I've been pondering both questions for a long time," Albert said. "The best I've been able to do in response to the first—how the Lord is able to change us—is come up with an analogy. Would you like to hear it?"

"Yes, absolutely."

"Very well. After we get a picture of how the Lord is able to change us, then we can ponder our part in the miracle—what we need to do to allow him to change us. Fair enough?"

Michael nodded.

"Okay, then." Albert stood up and walked over to the shelves next to the mantel. He pulled down a stack of papers. "Something else I've been working on," he said, as he came

back to the couch. "It's a little story I call *The King's Fields*—
my meager attempt to illustrate, at least by analogy, how the
Lord can heal us, and what is required of us in order to receive
that healing. I'll read just the first part of it to you. If you want
to stop me for any reason, of course, please speak up; I can be
an insufferable bore." Smiling, he adjusted his glasses and
started to read.

If you were to sail westward over the sea, and follow the signs in the heavens as you did so, you would
arrive at a field of red sand that spans the horizon.

Anciently, this beach was the site of a great battle
where a once glorious people were saved from destruction by a meek but mighty king. Their would-be con-
querors, skilled in the manner of war, fell upon them in
great fury, wielding blades tipped with sinister poisons.
These poisons weakened their victims' hearts before
depriving them of life, as the enemy sought to add to
their numbers by capturing the hearts of the people.
With each inflicted wound, the enemy gained control
of the victim's will.

For days the battle raged, and the defenders of the
land were weakening. A good number had been turned
to the enemy. Those who struggled to defend the land
were beginning to perish. Their bodies sagged and their
spirits wilted. Their muscles had withered to the point
that they could no longer grasp their swords and could

only barely lift their shields in defense. Their weakness had become so great that they almost would have done anything their enemies willed them to do.

At this critical point in the battle, the king—the lone unwounded soul—turned to look at his people. He barely recognized them. The mighty warriors he had fought with for ages now drooped and slumped and stumbled. Their skin sagged, and fear shown in their eyes. The king looked back at the host of his foes, who laughed almost in unison. Their victory was close at hand, and they rejoiced in it.

Only one hope remained for the king's people—a maneuver in warfare that had never before been tried, as no ruler under the heavens had ever had enough love or courage to do it. Even at this moment the king wished there was some other way. But another glance at his ever-weakening people told him there was not.

So the king turned back to the enemies who desired his weakness and death. And he dropped his shield to the ground.

An exultant cry pierced the air, and all the hosts of the enemy turned from their individual battles and rushed upon the defenseless king. They fell upon him in their full strength and fury, in order to end the battle for all time. They were confident that if he weakened, even in the slightest degree, there would be none to protect and heal his people. The battle would end in his and their deaths, and he and his people would be lost from under the heavens.

"But what could be gained by the king's action?" you might ask. "What would cause the king to make such an offering?"

A single hope upon which the fate of his entire people rested. You see, as the king opened himself to the weapons of the enemy, he took within himself the blades that had pierced the flesh and hearts of each of his people. If he could take each of those will-defeating blades within himself and yet remain pure, not yielding to the will of the enemy, he would overcome the poisons that had corrupted his people, and his pure heart would become the antidote to each and every poison.

The enemy rejoiced because no soul under heaven had ever been able to overcome their poisons. One blade's poison perhaps, or maybe two. But dozens or thousands? No. Millions or trillions? An impossibility. They needed only to capture the king's will and all would be over. So, thirsting for victory, they pierced the king's flesh and soul with every weapon they had used to weaken each of his people.

How long this torture continued no one can say. When the king lovingly roused his people back to consciousness, however, they witnessed a beach—once bright white—that now lay blood-red as far as the eye could see.

Although the people survived, their strength did not return. As long as the poison remained in their souls, their hearts and bodies remained weak.

"But the king can return their strength to them!" you might say.

Yes, but they had to let him. You see, the poison had a final debilitating effect: It induced those it had weakened to believe they were yet strong. The people's outward strength would return to them only as they came to recognize how weak they were within and then turned for strength to the only one in their kingdom who had uncorrupted strength to give.

However, how would they be able to see weakness they did not want to see? And what would invite them to look to another for strength when they wanted to believe in their own?

Albert took off his glasses and looked up.

Michael begged him to continue.

"That's probably enough for now," Albert replied. "The rest of the story would take us to matters we are not yet ready to discuss. But you asked how the Lord could heal and change us."

Michael nodded.

"I'm afraid that's the best this paltry mind can do. Broken

souls can be healed only by one who takes that brokenness upon himself but doesn't break. Having overcome the particular strains of brokenness that each of us suffers from, the unbroken one can then give us his victorious, unbroken will. This is precisely what the Savior has done for each of us. He suffered our pains, afflictions, and temptations, and took upon himself our sins and infirmities.[40] His suffering on our behalf was literally seared into his flesh.[41] Taking all of this upon and within himself, we have become 'members of his body, of his flesh, and of his bones.'[42] As Isaiah put it, 'he was wounded for our transgressions, he was bruised for our iniquities: the chastisement of our peace was upon him; and with his stripes we [may be] healed.'[43] 'I am able to make you holy,'[44] the Lord declares. But he will not—in fact, cannot[45]—do this for us unless we let him."

"Why wouldn't we let him?" Michael asked.

"Because, although unholy and therefore broken, we are not contrite, Michael. That is the problem. We are elder sons."

"Oh, yeah." Then Michael asked, "So how does the Lord reach elder sons who do not want to be reached?"

"That, my boy, is the question for which the gospel was designed to be the answer, a gospel that teaches us what we must do to allow the Lord to heal us and make us holy."

12

KNEE-BENDING RULES

Do you remember that story in the Old Testament where the Israelites were dying from wounds inflicted by fiery serpents?"[46]

Michael nodded. "They asked Moses to get the Lord to save them."

"Yes. So he approached the Lord about it and was told to make an image of the serpent out of brass and place it on the top of a pole. He was then promised that all those who looked to the image on the pole would be healed and saved."

"Kind of a strange story, if you ask me," Michael interjected. "Earlier it had been a great offense for the Israelites to make a graven image of a calf, yet here Moses is making a graven image of a serpent."

"It does seem odd, doesn't it?" Albert agreed. "But there's

an axiom I go by when reading the scriptures. That axiom is that the scriptures make sense. If something seems odd or isn't making sense to me, rather than dismiss it, I assume I'm simply lacking understanding. I know that if I keep poking and prodding and praying and pondering, my understanding will eventually be opened."

"Okay, so what sense have you made out of *this* story?"

"The Lord tells us that the brass serpent he had Moses place on the top of the pole was a type of the Lord himself,"[47] Albert answered. "All who looked to the serpent were saved, just as all who look to the Lord will be saved. If the brass serpent was a type, then it begs another question: To what might the fiery serpents themselves be a type?"

"The fiery serpents?" Michael asked. "The antagonists that bit Israel? In similitude of something?"

"It might help to remember that these antagonists, as you call them, prodded Israel to look to the Lord. Or, put another way, it was the fiery serpents that awakened within Israel the need to look to and rely upon another for salvation."

"So you're saying the fiery serpents weren't all bad?"

"It depends how you look at it," Albert answered. "On the one hand, people died from the serpents' wounds. But if you look at the story metaphorically, as we are invited to do by revelation, we see that the brass serpent Moses erected was in similitude of Christ. With that understanding, it is clear that the circumstances that invite us toward Christ are blessings to us spiritually even if they are challenges to us physically. Metaphorically speaking, the fiery serpents awakened Israel to their brokenness and motivated them to look toward a savior. Metaphorically, then, they were a blessing."

Michael nodded. "Interesting. I see that, yes." After a moment, he added, "So what does that have to do with us?"

"We have our own fiery serpents," Albert replied.

"You mean, like challenges?"

"I'm thinking of something else," Albert said, "although you're right that challenges can perform a similar function in our lives."

"Then what are you thinking of?" Michael asked.

"In order to ponder that, let's think again about the people of King Benjamin. What kind of people were they?"

"Good people, I think," Michael answered.

"Why do you think that?"

Michael recalled the images that had come to his mind as he read the night before. "I don't know," he shrugged. "For one thing, they went up to the temple to hear their king." He pictured their tents and the families huddling to listen to the sermon. "They seem conscientious and committed to trying to do good."

Albert nodded. "King Benjamin described his people in a similar way. He called them 'a diligent people in keeping the commandments of the Lord.'"[48] Albert picked up the Book of Mormon. "Remember that description as I read to you what happened to these people a few chapters later."

And now, it came to pass that when king Benjamin had made an end of speaking the words which had been delivered unto him by the angel of the Lord, that he cast his eyes round about on the multitude, and behold they had fallen to the earth, for the fear of the Lord had come upon them.

And they had viewed themselves in their own carnal state, even less than the dust of the earth. And they all cried aloud with one voice, saying: O have mercy, and apply the atoning blood of Christ that we may receive forgiveness of our sins, and our hearts may be purified.[49]

"I've always loved that," Michael said.

"Yes, but doesn't it puzzle you?"

"Puzzle me? Why?"

"What kind of people were these, Michael?" Albert asked again.

"A diligent people in keeping the commandments of the Lord," Michael repeated.

"So here we see the diligent commandment-keepers fallen to the ground, with the fear of the Lord upon them—not abject sinners, mind you, but good, conscientious, commandment-keeping people." Albert paused, and then asked, "Why? Why were they fallen?"

"Can I see the passage?" Michael asked, reaching toward Albert.

Albert handed him the book.

Michael studied the passage. "It says here that they viewed themselves in their own carnal state, even less than the dust of the earth." He looked up. "That's why they had fallen to the ground."

"Again, Michael, doesn't that strike you as odd?"

"Why odd?"

"That it's diligent commandment-keepers, not abject sinners, who recognize their own carnal natures. What does that suggest?"

Michael shrugged. "It sort of makes it seem like the commandments don't really matter." Then he chuckled and added, "Whether we keep them or whether we don't, we're toast."

"Actually, your second point is correct."

"That we're toast whether we keep them or not?" Michael asked incredulously.

"If *all* you do is keep the commandments, then yes," Albert nodded.

Michael's face puckered. "Then are you saying that the commandments don't matter?"

"On the contrary, my boy. There's almost nothing that matters more. For you see, in one important respect, the fiery serpents were symbolic of the commandments. It is the commandments that awaken us to our utter need for the Savior; they are our 'schoolmaster,' Paul said, 'to bring us unto Christ.'"[50]

The thought intrigued Michael. "How?"

"Now there's a question," Albert nodded. "In response, I'm going to share with you what I believe to be the central purpose of the commandments. However, what I'm about to say can be misunderstood if we're not careful. So after I mention it, we'll need to explore what it does and doesn't mean. Fair enough?"

Michael nodded.

"Okay, then, here it is: As I read the scriptures, I find there are two main purposes for the commandments, one of which is well understood and one of which is not. The first is that the commandments teach us the standards of heaven. They prepare us for heaven by teaching us to live and be refined by heaven's law in the here and now, a law lived by Christ and by all who will live with him in the eternities. Agreed?"

Michael nodded.

"Here's the part that's not so well understood: Because the commandments teach us the standards of heaven, they also awaken us to the realization of how we are failing fully to live those standards. And since forgiveness for such failures cannot be found in the commandments themselves, the commandments therefore drive us to Christ with broken hearts and contrite spirits. This, Jesus taught, is one of their primary purposes. To the Nephites he said, 'I have given you the law and the commandments of my Father, that ye shall believe in me, and that ye shall repent of your sins, and come unto me with a broken heart and a contrite spirit.'[51]

"The people of King Benjamin are a great example of this purpose in action. Knowing how important the commandments were, when they recognized their failure fully to keep them, they threw themselves in fear at the Lord's feet, begging for his mercy.[52] As you will recall from the story, he then changed their hearts, that they had no more disposition to do evil,[53] which is to say that he prepared a way for them to be able to live what he had commanded them.[54] It was the law—or, specifically, their own brokenness exposed by the law—that drove them to Christ for healing."

Albert looked at Michael for a moment, gauging the level of comprehension in his eyes. "Let's see how the commandments might invite the same reaction in us as they did in the people of King Benjamin." He stood up and retrieved a second set of scriptures from the shelf next to the mantel.

Taking his seat again and opening the book, he said, "Let's consider a few of Jesus' teachings. I'm in 3 Nephi 12, beginning at verse 21." Michael quickly turned there.

Ye have heard that it hath been said by them of old time, and it is also written before you, that thou shalt not kill, and whosoever shall kill shall be in danger of the judgment of God.[55]

Albert looked up. "That's an expression of the outward law—thou shalt not kill. In this case it might be a law you find easy to keep. But the Lord didn't leave it there. Listen to the next verse."

> But I say unto you, that whosoever is angry with his brother shall be in danger of his judgment. And whosoever shall say to his brother, Raca, shall be in danger of the council; and whosoever shall say, Thou fool, shall be in danger of hell fire.[56]

Albert looked back up at Michael. "Are you still feeling as comfortable?"

Michael looked back down at the verses in the scriptures he was using. He recalled some of the harsh things he had said to his father over the years. The English equivalents of "Raca" were never far from his mind and all too often escaped his lips. The verse convicted him. "Not as much, no," he answered quietly. "Then again, I'm not sure it would leave anyone with much room for comfort."

"Indeed," Albert agreed. "Which is entirely the point."

Michael looked up at him.

Albert continued. "Perhaps here you find a commandment you are not fully living—a commandment that says, in effect, 'Thou shalt not become angry.' Perhaps as you read this verse you begin to worry, for you know that 'the Lord cannot look upon sin with the least degree of allowance,'[57] and yet here you find a commandment you are not fully living. Perhaps you can feel yourself crying from deep inside, 'But Lord, I get angry.' If you listen carefully, you may feel or hear a response that goes something like this: 'Yes, my child, you do; but I don't. Come unto me and be healed.'

"The commandments we are struggling to live," Albert continued, "are located precisely at the fault line between our developing holiness and our still carnal natures. These commandments expose our remaining, ample and damning brokenness, every one of them inviting us to view ourselves in our own carnal state and to contritely fall to the ground in fear of the Lord. If you and I are not completely clean and pure, and we're not, then the commandments compel us, just as they compelled the commandment-keeping people of King Benjamin, to our knees. And not merely to our knees, but to our knees before Him, which is the difference between despair on the one hand and hope on the other; for the Lord can change us."[58]

Michael had felt a hint of despair pressing in, but this comment pulled him free. *Seeing problems in myself is only cause for despair so long as I insist on the fiction of being problem free on my own!* he realized. *But that is pure pride—pride masquerading as forlorn humility, perhaps, but pride nonetheless. To kneel before Him is to find hope.*

"Here's another example just a few verses later," Albert continued.

> Behold, it is written by them of old time, that thou shalt not commit adultery.[59]

"That's the outward law," Albert commented, "'thou shalt not commit adultery.' But again, the Lord doesn't stop there."

But I say unto you, that whosoever looketh on a woman, to lust after her, hath committed adultery already in his heart. Behold, I give unto you a commandment, that ye suffer none of these things to enter into your heart. For it is better that ye should deny yourselves of these things, wherein ye will take up your cross, than that ye should be cast into hell.[60]

Michael looked down, not out of despair but out of fear. His thoughts weren't always pure, and he sometimes viewed and thought about things he knew he shouldn't. He hoped Albert wouldn't notice the blush he felt rising in his cheeks and heating up his ears. *But I don't have a problem,* he insisted to himself.

"You see," Albert said, "the Lord can redeem us from our sins, but he cannot redeem one who fails to see the sins from which he needs to be redeemed."

The comment challenged Michael's internal defense. He looked up at Albert. *Does he know?*

"You almost certainly will never commit the outward sin of adultery," Albert continued, "and for your sake, Michael, I pray to God that you don't, but how are you doing on the deeper gospel? Do you ever look at things you shouldn't? Do you ever have thoughts you shouldn't? Are your desires at all impure?"

Michael buried his chin again in his chest.

"Or, for that matter," Albert went on, "do you ever run afoul of the first of the Ten Commandments? Do you ever prioritize other things before the Lord—your hobbies, for example, your recreation, your home, your work? Do you forgive from your heart those who trespass against you? Are you ever envious? Resentful? Are you filled with charity? Meekness? Mercy? Do you honor your parents?"[61]

Michael began to cower at the litany of the commandments Albert was mentioning. He began to lose heart once again. "But no one is keeping all of those things perfectly," he protested.

"Exactly!" Albert responded. "'The law entered,' in the words of the Apostle Paul, 'that the offence might abound,' so that 'all the world may become guilty before God.'[62] That's the point, Michael! Listen to Alma's words to his son, Corianton." He opened the Book of Mormon and began to read.

> Now, how could a man repent except he should sin? How could he sin if there was no law? How could there be a law save there was a punishment?
>
> Now, there was a punishment affixed, and a just law given, which brought remorse of conscience unto man.[63]

"So you see, Michael, by teaching us the law of God and exposing within us the places we are failing to fully live that law, the commandments bring 'remorse of conscience unto man,' awakening within us the need to look for deliverance to Him who was raised up on a pole.[64] 'Therefore we conclude,' Paul wrote, 'that a man is justified [or reconciled to God] by faith without the deeds of the law.'[65] To which Paul then asked this rhetorical question: 'Do we then make void the law through faith?' His response? 'God forbid: yea, we establish the law.'[66] It is the law that brings us to the One who can straighten our crookedness and justify us before God. Another way to say it is that while the commandments prepare us for heaven, they do not on their own make us heavenly, nor do they qualify us for heaven. Rather, they awaken us to our imperfections and thereby invite us to come humbly to Christ. It is then the Lord who 'makes weak things become strong unto [us]' and transforms us into beings whose dispositions have been changed in such a way that the heavenly law becomes 'written in our hearts.'[67]

"This is what Lehi was talking about when he said,

By the law no flesh is justified; or, by the law men are cut off. . . . Wherefore, redemption cometh in and through the Holy Messiah. . . . Behold, he offereth himself a sacrifice for sin, to answer the ends of the law, unto all those who have a broken heart and a contrite spirit.[68]

"He couldn't have said it plainer, could he?" Albert concluded.

Michael was feeling burdened by the weight of his sins. The thought that he might be systematically overlooking his sins worried him even more. He thought of the Israelites who had been bitten and were threatened with death. *To wallow in despair over my sinfulness is tantamount to the Israelites lying down to die rather than looking up to be healed by the Being that was raised up on the pole to save them,* he chided himself. *I have to look to Him.*

"Have you ever wondered why the Lord in the Garden of Eden gave Adam and Eve two commandments that couldn't both be kept at the same time?" Albert asked.

Michael looked up. "As a matter of fact, yes. I've wondered that many times. I've thought maybe it was in order to allow them to exercise agency. The Lord wouldn't cast innocent souls out of his presence; he allowed them to make a choice."

Albert nodded. "You might consider an additional reason as well. In light of what we've been talking about, why else might the Lord have given to Adam and Eve commandments they couldn't keep perfectly?"

Words Albert had quoted from Paul rang in Michael's ears. *"The law entered, that the offence might abound,"* so that *"all the world may become guilty before God,"*[69] therefore compelling them to look to a savior for deliverance. And then Michael understood. "The only way Adam and Eve could progress from an immortal state of naive innocence to an eternal state of purified holiness," he heard himself say, "was through a Savior who could make them holy. Alone, no commandments in the Garden could have taken them beyond the Garden." Michael's jaw dropped. For years, all he had seen around this question had been darkness, and all of a sudden there was light. From his own lips.

"Yes. And what compelled them to turn to the Savior?"

"Their transgression of the law," Michael nodded. "Their brokenness under the law awakened them to their need for a Savior—a Savior who could then take them far beyond where they had been."

Albert smiled. "That's right, Michael; that's the way it seems to me anyway. What is true for us was true from the very beginning. Although before their transgression Adam and Eve, unlike us, were innocent, they, *like* us, were not yet holy. Without sin, Lehi taught, 'they would have remained in a state of innocence [but would have had] no joy'; knowing no sin, they would not have been able to do good.[70] Adam and Eve had to progress from a state of immortal innocence *from sin* to a state of eternal holiness that *would never countenance* sin. In order for this purification process to happen, sin itself had to be overcome.

"So from this perspective the law was introduced, as Lehi, Paul, Alma, and countless other prophets have taught, in order to introduce sin,[71] 'that the offense might abound,' making man 'guilty before God,' so that Adam and Eve, and we in similitude of them, would come to the Lord with broken hearts and contrite spirits. The promise is that the Savior, whose nature is itself enmity against sin,[72] will then not only cover our sins but also expunge from us the desire for sin.[73] Through the grace and power of his atonement, he will sanctify us in him, that we become not just innocent but holy,[74] possessors of attributes of godliness."[75]

Albert continued, "When we, like the people of King Benjamin, and Adam and Eve before them, become awakened to our brokenness under the law and throw ourselves contritely at the Lord's feet, he will make our scarlet sins as snow and purify our broken hearts, that we, too, may be changed by the Spirit into beings that 'have no more disposition to do evil, but to do good continually.'"[76]

"Which brings us," he added, "to the central, contrition-inviting hub of the commandments: the sin-exposing commandment of the Sabbath."

13

THE SABBATH CREATION

This is what the Sabbath is about?" Michael asked. "About our brokenness and our contrition? I thought it was about rest."

"Indeed it is, Michael. But do you know what *rest* is?"

"I know I'd like more of it," Michael joked.

"You mean more rest from your physical labors?"

"Yes, just like the Lord rested during the seventh period of creation."

"Tell me what happened on the seventh day of creation," Albert invited.

"Well, nothing happened; isn't that the point?" Michael replied. "The Lord rested on the seventh day from all his labors."

"Let me read something to you," Albert said. "This is from

section 77 of the Doctrine and Covenants, verse 12. Here the Prophet Joseph asks a question of the Lord regarding the sounding of the trumpets mentioned in the book of Revelation. This was the Lord's answer."

> As God made the world in six days, and on the seventh day he finished his work, and sanctified it, and also formed man out of the dust of the earth, even so, in the beginning of the seventh thousand years will the Lord God sanctify the earth, and complete the salvation of man.[77]

"Does that say that man was formed in the flesh on the seventh day rather than the sixth?" Michael asked.

"Curious, isn't it," Albert replied. "That's never what I've believed, but this verse does make it sound that way. If you read the creation accounts in Genesis, Moses, and Abraham, you will see that each of those accounts could be read to say the same thing.[78] Other scriptures, though, can be read to imply otherwise."

"So what do *you* think?" Michael asked.

"On balance, I'm not sure, and I suppose it doesn't matter too much to me which day man was formed on the earth. However, I think another idea in this verse matters a lot."

"What's that?"

"Think first about what the Lord is doing in the verse. He is making an analogy between the events that will occur in the beginning of the <u>seventh period of the earth's his</u>tory and the events that occurred on the <u>seventh day of the earth's creation.</u> The Lord said that on the seventh day he sanctified his work, just as he will sanctify the earth at the beginning of the seventh period of its history. If that is true, and this verse seems to leave no room for doubt, then <u>it isn't the case that the Lord did noth-ing on the seventh day</u>. Far from it. He says here that while he made the world in six days, he sanctified his work on the seventh day. The seventh day—what we now commemorate through the Sabbath—was the <u>day he brought man into the presence of God.</u>"

"But that means the Lord didn't rest on the seventh day," Michael said.

"That depends on what is meant by the word *rest*."

"So what does it mean?" Michael asked.

"On the seventh day," Albert continued, "after the earth had been completed, who was on the earth?"

"Adam and Eve. Along with all the animals, of course."

"And who else?"

"Who else?"

Albert nodded.

"God?" Michael asked.

"Exactly. The <u>earth was created for the purpose of bringing man into the presence of God</u>—or, in the language of the scriptures, <u>into God's 'rest.'</u>"[79]

LOVING THE HOLY SABBATH

Michael remembered that he knew this. "Rest" in the scriptures is often a reference to God's presence.

"All of the Lord's work over the first six days of the
creation," Albert continued, "was in order to enable the work
of the seventh day—the labor of bringing man into his presence. The story of the creation is therefore the story of how the
Lord did not then, and will not now, rest from his redeeming
labor until all who are willing are brought into the presence of
God."

Michael pondered this. "Is there a connection between the
rest that means the presence of God and the *rest* that means a
break from labor?"

Albert nodded. "I think so, yes. The Lord *did* rest from his
work upon completing the labor of sanctification on the seventh day. However, he rested because his work of bringing man
into God's presence had been completed for a season—that is,
until the fall. In his letter to the Hebrews, Paul wrote, 'For he
that is entered into his rest, he also hath ceased from his own
works, as God did from his.'[80] But then he added, 'Let us
labour therefore to enter into that rest.'[81]

"So the command to rest on the Sabbath is not a command
simply to take a break from our physical labors. The creation
story tells us that there is much work to do in order to obtain
the rest of the Lord. We rest from our physical labors in order to
turn our attention to the Lord's labor on our behalf and to
awaken us to the realization that we need to rest from every

practice that is unholy or impure[82]—every labor in our lives that will keep us from him. We are to fill our Sabbaths with sanctifying pursuits that will prepare us for God's presence, and 'never be weary of good works,' as Alma instructed his son, Helaman, but 'be meek and lowly in heart; for such shall find rest to their souls.'"[83]

"That sounds like a call for a broken heart and contrite spirit," Michael observed.

"Indeed. Here's what the Lord said about that." Albert opened in the Doctrine and Covenants to section 59.

> Thou shalt offer a sacrifice unto the Lord thy God in righteousness, even that of a broken heart and a contrite spirit. And that thou mayest more fully keep thyself unspotted from the world, thou shalt go to the house of prayer and offer up thy sacraments upon my holy day; for verily this is a day appointed unto you to rest from your labors, and to pay thy devotions unto the Most High; nevertheless thy vows shall be offered up in righteousness on all days and at all times; but remember that on this, the Lord's day, thou shalt offer thine oblations and thy sacraments unto the Most High, confessing thy sins unto thy brethren, and before the Lord.[84]

"We are to offer up our vows or commitments on all days," Albert said, "but the Sabbath is specifically set apart as a day where we offer our oblations—that is, our offerings of time, talent, contrition, and so on—and confess our sins to others and before the Lord. It is a day that is blessed and hallowed to prepare us for the rest of the Lord,[85] being designed to bring about contrition within us, just as it did within Adam and Eve, by awakening us to our sins."

"How?" Michael asked.

"In order to address that question, let us consider two heaven-sent prayers."

14

A DAY OF CONTRITION

The sacrament prayers?" Michael guessed.

"Have you ever pondered them?" Albert asked.

Michael thought about it for a moment and then shook his head. "Pondering would be a bit strong, I'm afraid."

"If you had, you might have seen what we've been discussing."

Michael leaned forward. "How so?"

"Let's ask that question of the prayers." Albert stood up and walked over to the end table to Michael's right. From the drawer, he pulled a few pieces of paper.

Taking his seat again, he said, "I think you'll see a few interesting things in the prayers—patterns of similarity and difference, for example. In order to see them though, it will help transcribe the prayers in a way that makes the patterns obvious."

"Okay," Michael said.

Albert opened to the twentieth section of the Doctrine and Covenants.[86] "This is going to take me a minute."

"No problem. Take your time."

Albert diagrammed the prayers and handed the first to Michael.

THE PRAYER ON THE BREAD

O God, the Eternal Father, we ask thee in the name of thy Son, Jesus Christ, to bless and sanctify this bread to the souls of all those who partake of it,

1. that they may
   a. eat in remembrance of the body of thy Son, and
   b. witness unto thee, O God, the Eternal Father, that they are willing to
      • take upon them the name of thy Son, and
      • always remember him, and
      • keep his commandments which he has given them;
2. that they may
   → always have his Spirit to be with them.

Amen.

"What do you notice?" Albert said.

Michael asked about the significance of the squares.

"We'll get there in a bit. What else do you see?"

"How about the circle?"

"That will make sense when we look at the water prayer. But what else do you notice—in the structure?"

Michael studied the prayer's pattern. "Ah, it's a covenant, isn't it?"

Albert smiled and nodded. "Meaning what?"

As a lawyer, this was something Michael knew much about, as his work was largely the negotiation of deals that consisted of covenants or promises between parties. "The prayer is constructed as an agreement." Michael looked more closely at it. "Our side is number 1: We witness our willingness to do three things—to take upon us the name of Christ, to always remember him, and to keep his commandments."

"And in return, the Lord promises what?" Albert asked.

"Number 2—that we will have his Spirit to be with us."

"How often?"

"Always," Michael answered.

"Now, let's compare that to the water prayer," Albert said. He handed the second sheet of paper to Michael.

THE PRAYER ON THE WATER

O God, the Eternal Father, we ask thee in the name of thy Son, Jesus Christ, to bless and sanctify this water to the souls of all those who drink of it,

    1. that they may

        a. do it in remembrance of the blood of thy Son, which was shed for them; that they may

        b. witness unto thee, O God, the Eternal Father, that they do

            ♦

            ♦ always remember him,

            ♦

    2. that they may

    → ◯ have his Spirit to be with them.

Amen.

Michael looked at the two prayers. "There's no 'always' in the promise of the Spirit in the water prayer," he observed. "The circle is blank."

"That's correct. What else is different?"

"Well, whereas we witness our *willingness* to do three things in the bread prayer, in the water prayer we don't witness to our willingness but to whether we actually do something."

"That something being what?" Albert asked.

"That we do always remember him."

Albert nodded.

Michael continued. "And then there are two things that were mentioned in the bread prayer that are specifically omitted from the water prayer—our taking upon us the name of Christ and keeping his commandments."

"So what do you suppose is the significance of those differences?" Albert asked.

After thinking about it, Michael shook his head. "I'm not sure."

"Let's start with the bread or body prayer, then, shall we?" Albert suggested.

"Okay."

"You said it's a covenant."

Michael nodded. "Yes."

"The Lord's promise to us is that we will always have his Spirit to be with us."

"Yes," Michael agreed, "so long as we take his name upon us, always remember him, and keep his commandments."

"That's his promise to us—that if we do those three things we will always have his Spirit with us?" Albert asked.

"That's what it looks like to me," Michael answered.

"Do you always have his Spirit with you, Michael?"

Michael wasn't fully prepared for the question. Truth was, he often felt alienated from the Spirit and spiritually alone. Notwithstanding his experience with Albert's talk, for example, most Church meetings felt dull to him. Between struggling to keep the kids quiet and sermons that were delivered by well-meaning but unskilled members of the ward, he only rarely felt recharged by what happened at church. His personal prayers also mostly felt habitual and wooden. In fact, he couldn't remember the last time he felt like he'd received an actual answer to prayer. *I think I've felt the Spirit more in the past two days than I've felt it in years,* he thought in response. The realization both depressed him and gave him hope. He looked back at Albert. "No, not always."

"Then what does the bread prayer tell you about those times you don't have the Spirit?" Albert asked.

Michael puzzled over the question. He looked down and reread the prayer. "Oh," he reacted, "I get it. It tells me that if I don't have the Spirit it's because I haven't done one or more of the three things I covenanted to do."

"Exactly. Since the Lord doesn't lie, I can know for a surety that if the Spirit isn't with me, it's because I haven't kept something on my side of the covenant. Either I haven't taken his name upon me, I haven't remembered him, or I haven't kept his commandments."

Michael nodded.

"Which brings us to the water prayer. Notice, first of all, what's missing in the last line."

Michael glanced again at the water prayer. "The word *always,*" he answered.

"Why do you suppose it's missing? It's in the bread prayer; why not here too?"

Michael thought about that. *Why does the water prayer seem to promise less than the bread prayer? I'm glad to have the Spirit, like the water prayer says, but I'd prefer to have it always like the bread prayer promises.* Then he realized: *But I* DON'T *have it always.* He looked at the prayers again. *Of course! We're promised in the first prayer that we can have the Spirit always, so long as we keep our side of the covenant. But of course we don't keep those terms perfectly, and because of that, we lose the promised companionship of the Spirit as well!*

Suddenly, the water prayer took on new and significant meaning. *Maybe the blessing over the water is about how we can get the abundance of the Spirit back, despite our weaknesses and failures. We've blown the terms of the covenant and have lost the Spirit as a result. However, the Lord in his grace, through the blood that he shed for us, offers us the way to receive that abundance once again.*

Michael leaned back in his chair. "Wow!"

"What are you seeing?" Albert asked.

"I think I get it—one way to interpret the difference in the prayers, anyway. The bread prayer is a statement of the covenant, the terms of which we all, to one degree or another, fail fully to keep. Therefore, by the terms of that covenant, we have no right to the constant companionship of the Spirit. But through the offering of his blood, Christ created the way for us to get that Spirit back! The water prayer can therefore be read as a statement of the covenant of repentance and forgiveness, made possible by the Savior's atoning blood."

Albert smiled and nodded. "Although that's what I have believed," he said, "I have to admit I've never expressed it so clearly."

"It still leaves a mystery though," Michael said. "I see why the word *always* is omitted in the water prayer, but what about these other two omissions?" he asked, pointing at the prayer. "There's nothing listed about taking the name of Christ on us or keeping the commandments, both of which are listed as requirements in the bread prayer."

"Yes," Albert said. "Why do you think that would be?"

Michael thought about it. "I'm not sure," he finally replied.

"As for the question of taking upon us the name of Christ, there's something else we need to see in the prayers in order to address it. But we are prepared to address the other point—the omission in the water prayer of any reference to keeping the commandments. Shall we think about that one for a moment?"

Michael nodded. "Please."

"If you had to witness in the bread prayer that you do, in fact, keep his commandments, Michael, would you be able to so witness?"

Michael thought about it and shook his head.

"That's the point. No one would be able to do it. Our problem is precisely that we haven't fully kept his command-ments—we've struggled with anger, for example, or resentment, or we've viewed things we shouldn't and have entertained impure thoughts. And so on. We have failed to fully keep his commandments. That is why, in my opinion, we need to repent and get the constant companionship of the Spirit back."

"I see. You're suggesting that the water prayer doesn't contain a declaration that we keep his commandments because our problem is precisely that we haven't been keeping those commandments."

"Exactly."

Michael looked back down at the prayers. "Then how is it that we can make the declaration that we 'do always remember him' when in fact we haven't?"

"Here's what I think," Albert said. "We don't declare that we *have* always remembered him. You are quite right that we couldn't honestly make that declaration. Rather, we make a declaration about the present moment—the moment we are contemplating the sacrament. Realizing that we have sometimes forgotten him, we contritely express that it is our present desire and intention to remember him always."

"Oh, I see," Michael said, relaxing back in his chair once more. "It's an expression of our repentance."

"That's the way it seems to me," Albert agreed.

Michael sat in silence for a few moments, letting everything settle in. "So the sacrament prayers remind us of our brokenness," he summarized.

Albert nodded. "By making the keeping of the commandments a condition of having his Spirit always, the prayers bring us square up against our brokenness and therefore offer us the opportunity to contritely see our sins."

"Yes, I can see that," Michael replied.

"The question, Michael, is whether we can feel it. Unless and until we see it from our souls, we will not find rest at the thought of meeting our Lord and Savior. The Sabbath was set apart as a day to find that rest—rest from unholy thoughts, words, deeds, priorities, and desires that keep us from Him. It is a day of rest from the labors of sin, a day for us prodigals to 'come to ourselves' and see how we have attached ourselves to another and journeyed far away from our father and his house. Like the prodigal in that moment, or the people of King Benjamin when they saw themselves in their own carnal state, the Sabbath is designed to bring us to our knees before the Lord. With King Benjamin's people, we cry: 'O have mercy, and apply the atoning blood of Christ that we may receive forgiveness of our sins, and our hearts may be purified.'"[87]

Albert paused and looked at Michael. "And when you do this, you will discover, just as the young prodigal did, that you have been missing someone you can't afford to miss."

Michael waited for Albert to continue. "Who?"

"Your father."

15

RETURNING HOME

Michael's mood instantly darkened. "My father?" he sneered. "What does *he* have to do with the Sabbath day?"

"More than you know," Albert answered.

"How?"

Albert reached for the Bible and opened it to Luke 15. "Perhaps it's time that we actually *looked* at the parable of the prodigals." He smiled at Michael. Offering the book to him, he said, "notice how the parable begins in verse 11 with a statement about father and sons."

Michael looked at the verse and reluctantly nodded.

"This relationship is reiterated in the next verse, verse 12, where the younger son asks for his inheritance."

Michael read the verse and nodded once more.

"Do you notice anything unusual in that verse?" Albert asked.

Michael read the verse again, a little less begrudgingly than before.

> And the younger of them said to his father, Father, give me the portion of goods that falleth to me. And he divided unto them his living.[88]

"I suppose it's interesting that although only the younger son asked for his inheritance it seems like the elder son received his as well, as it says that 'he divided unto *them* his living.'"

"Hmm, that *is* interesting," Albert agreed. "I'd not noticed that before."

"So you're talking about something else?"

"Yes. Actually, you just mentioned it without realizing how odd it is."

Michael wondered what he had said.

"Think about what's happening here," Albert said. "These sons are getting their inheritance."

"Right," Michael nodded.

"Doesn't that seem odd?"

"Odd?" Michael reacted. "Why?"

"When does a child normally receive his inheritance, Michael?"

"After his parents have—" he stopped. *Of course!* Michael thought to himself. *We inherit after our parents have died, but here the sons inherit while their father is still alive.* "The younger son asked for his inheritance while his father was still living." Michael's voice trailed off.

"Precisely. And if he wants his inheritance while his father is still alive, that means that to him, his father is essentially what?"

"Dead." The word descended from Michael's lips like a hammer into his soul. For his own father was dead to him— had been for years, in fact—even while living. His last breath was a mere formality, and a longed-for one at that.

"Notice the word the Savior puts into the younger son's mouth," Albert continued. "'Father, give me the portion of goods that falleth to me.'"

"Falleth," Michael repeated. "Is it possible that hearkens to the fall of man?"

"It may," Albert nodded. "I believe the parable can be read that way, anyway, with all that implies. For example, notice how after the repeated mention of the father-son relationship in the first two verses of the parable, the story then goes silent about the father—and, for that matter, about the young man's status as a son—until the moment the younger son 'came to himself' in verse 17."

Michael looked down and scanned the verses. Sure enough, after the son collected what "fell" to him, what had been a father-son narrative changed dramatically into the story of a lone, solitary soul.

"The man might as well have been fatherless," Albert continued, "as his father came to play no role in his life. In that respect, the young man wasn't really even a son in any meaningful respect. Dead to his father, he was dead as a child as well. His story didn't change until he looked again to his father and was born again as a son. From that point on, the father-son relationship becomes central again in every verse."

Albert paused and looked at Michael. "Which suggests what about us?"

Michael sat motionless. He had become derailed by what he thought he heard between the lines of Albert's words: that being dead to one's father is tantamount to a fall from grace. He was picturing his father in his hospital bed in Hackensack. *The choices he made destroyed our family,* he defended himself. *And has he even once acknowledged it?* Michael resolutely shook his head. *No! He's never reached out to me—not once, not ever! He's never once even called me.* He thought of his father reaching his arm to him. Michael clenched his teeth. *And now he wants me to come running to his bedside?*

"I'm sorry Al," Michael said without looking up. "I don't think I can do that."

"Do what, my boy?"

"What you want me to do—return as the prodigal to my father."

"You think I'm talking about your earthly father?"

Michael looked up at him in surprise. "You're not?"

"No. Not yet anyway. I'm speaking of a different father."

Michael's mood brightened. "Heavenly Father?"

"Let me read you something," Albert said. He opened the Book of Mormon. "I'm in the Book of Alma. The lawyer Zeezrom is questioning Amulek. Here is what he asks."

> Now Zeezrom saith again unto him: Is the Son of God the very Eternal Father?[89]

Albert looked up at Michael. "How would you answer Zeezrom's question?"

"I would say he was on the right track, but that he was confusing the Son with the Father—that our Heavenly Father is actually the very Eternal Father."

Albert nodded. "Let me read you Amulek's answer."

> And Amulek said unto him: Yea, he is the very Eternal Father of heaven and of earth, and all things which in them are; he is the beginning and the end, the first and the last; and he shall come into the world to redeem his people; and he shall take upon him the transgressions of those who believe on his name; and these are they that shall have eternal life, and salvation cometh to none else.[90]

"Amulek is saying that Christ is the very Eternal Father?" Michael questioned.

"That's what he is saying, yes."

"Can that be right?"

Albert laughed. "You want to edit him?"

Michael smiled and shook his head. "No, I'm just wondering if the context paints a different picture, that's all."

"Well, here's what Abinadi said about it." Albert turned to the book of Mosiah.

> Teach them that redemption cometh through Christ the Lord, who is the very Eternal Father.[91]

"I thought Heavenly Father was our Eternal Father," Michael said.

"Indeed he is."

"But that's not what those verses seem to be saying," Michael replied.

"These verses are saying nothing about what Heavenly Father is or isn't. You and I both know he is the father of our spirits and is therefore rightfully called our 'Heavenly Father.' These scriptures are simply saying that Christ can also be called our father—in fact, that he is rightfully called our 'very Eternal Father.'"

"That's the part I don't understand."

Albert went silent for a moment. "Perhaps it would help to ponder fatherhood for a moment. When your first child, Hayden, was born," he said, "you were considered his father. Why is that?"

"Because I was his biological parent, I suppose," he said.

"The father of his body," Albert followed up.

"Yes."

"So the father of a person's body is said to be the 'father' of that person?"

"Yes."

"If Helen and I had adopted, although I wouldn't have been the child's biological father, I would have been accounted his father under the laws of adoption."

Michael nodded.

"And having been accounted his father, he would have taken on my surname, which is what connects a child with his father in the minds and institutions of the public."

Michael nodded again.

"So whoever gives a child either his body or his name, or both, is said to be that child's father."

Michael thought about it. "That would be right, yes."

"Since Hayden received both his body and his name from you, you were his father on both counts."

Michael was beginning to feel like he was being cross-examined. "Yes," he agreed.

"And of course, since Heavenly Father, as the father of Hayden's spirit, is also rightly called his father, the father of a person's spirit is *also* considered a father," Albert summarized.

"Yes," Michael agreed again. "But what are you driving at, Al?"

"I want us to be clear about what makes someone a father.

So far we've agreed that whoever gives you your body and/or your spirit and/or your name can be said to be your father."

Michael thought about it. "I agree with that, yes."

"Now, look at the words I drew squares around in the prayer on the bread."

Michael picked up the sheet of paper and looked at the words. He blinked and looked at them again.

"What words do you see?"

"Body, name, and Spirit," he answered, trying to process the implications.

"The very things that make one someone's child," Albert nodded. "And from whom do we receive all three?"

Then Michael saw it. His mind raced to put details to the answer he knew was the truth. *Because of the Savior's resurrection, we will receive a perfected, immortal body. And we take upon ourselves his name through baptism, and then he blesses us with his Spirit through the gift of the Holy Ghost, which enables our spirits to be born into a new life, a blessing that is renewed in the sacrament prayers.* [92] These revelations filled Michael with wonder. "He really does, doesn't he?" he said. "Christ gives us all three."

"Yes, he does," Albert replied. "You see, the sacrament is the ordinance of our rebirth as children of Christ. Because of the labor that produced the blood referenced in the prayer on the water, as we remember him and repent of all the ways we have failed to keep his commandments, we receive his Spirit. Which Spirit comes, Mormon taught, 'because of meekness and lowliness of heart,' and which Spirit is the power by which we become sanctified from the desire for sin.[93]

"The Savior declared, 'I am he who was prepared from the foundation of the world to redeem my people. Behold, I am Jesus Christ. I am the Father and the Son. In me shall all mankind have life, and that eternally, even they who shall believe on my name; and they shall become my sons and my daughters.'[94]

"This rebirth in Christ is precisely what King Benjamin emphasized to his people. Listen to what he said:

> And now, because of the covenant which ye have made ye shall be called the children of Christ, his sons, and his daughters; for behold, this day he hath spiritually begotten you; for ye say that your hearts are changed through faith on his name; therefore, ye are born of him and have become his sons and his daughters.[95]

"So you see, Michael, the Sabbath is designed both to awaken us to our sins and to turn our hearts and minds contritely in remembrance to our Father—both to our Heavenly Father and to the Creator or Father of eternal life. The everlasting Father,'[96] the Lord Jesus Christ. If we come unto him contritely, remembering our sins and his ability to forgive and turn us from them, he will change our hearts until, like the people of King Benjamin, 'we have no more disposition to do evil, but to do good continually.'[97] Then, with the people of

King Benjamin, we will be 'called the children of Christ, his sons and his daughters.' We will then not only have taken his name upon us but will have had it written in our hearts."⁹⁸

"That's the willingness to take his name upon us that we witness to in the prayer on the bread, isn't it?" Michael asked.

"It starts with our expression of willingness," Albert replied, "but his name becomes written and sealed in our hearts as we continually remember him and allow our hearts to be changed through his Spirit. That is the miracle the Sabbath is designed to bring about in us, a miracle so important that the Lord established the Sabbath as a sign of that miracle through the generations." Albert opened the Bible to the book of Exodus. "Listen to what the Lord told Moses:

> Speak thou . . . unto the children of Israel, saying, Verily my sabbaths ye shall keep: for it is a sign between me and you throughout your generations; that ye may know that I am the Lord that doth sanctify you.⁹⁹

Albert paused and then said, "So the Sabbath was established that we might know that it is the Lord that sanctifies us. It is a commemoration of his labor on our behalf, the labor of creation or birth that shapes us into his children—that is, into beings who belong in his presence. As we, like the prodigal, turn from every unholy practice and observe to keep the Sabbath day, we signal our desire and willingness to be sanctified. The Lord, like the father in the parable, waits, looking across the gulf of our brokenness for the sign of our turning. And then, when we turn toward him, he comes rushing to welcome, renew, and refresh us."[100]

"What do you mean by the sign of our turning?" Michael asked.

"True contrition comes with a sign," Albert responded.

"Which is what?"

"If you are serious about that question, Michael, it's time you start thinking about what's keeping you from Hackensack."

16

BURDENS

Michael bristled. "What's keeping me from Hackensack is a father who cares about no one but himself."

"Does he resemble anyone else in that regard?"

Michael's eyes narrowed. "You mean me?"

"Or me," Albert said, nonchalantly.

"He doesn't resemble you at all," Michael responded angrily.

"Okay, then how about you?"

Twenty years of heartache ripped through Michael's soul—the drinking, the indifference, the absence, the shallowness, the breaking up of the family. "I'm sorry, Albert," he said stiffly, "I'm certainly not perfect, but I'm unlike him in almost every respect."

"Actually, Michael, if you're not perfect, you're exactly like him in the only respect that really matters." He handed Michael the Bible, opened to James, chapter 2. "Go ahead and read verse 10."

Michael was suddenly tired of the scriptures. The thought of another verse telling him what a problem he had filled him with dread. Reluctantly, he took the book from Albert and started to read.

> For whosoever shall keep the whole law, and yet offend in one point, he is guilty of all.[101]

"Rubbish," Michael said as he tossed the book on the table in front of him. "Pure rubbish."

"You disagree?"

"With my whole soul."

"I see. So you think a little bit of unredeemed brokenness is okay."

"Compared to a whole *lot* of unredeemed brokenness, yes, I do."

"So only the dreadfully broken need a Savior, is that it? Those who are a little less broken can work things out on their own."

Michael heard the absurdity in Albert's words, but his mind was made up. "I'd rather go to hell than go to Hackensack," he blurted. "It doesn't matter what you say. And if that's what's required for heaven, I guess I'm just not cut out for it."

"Hell or Hackensack," Albert said, attempting a joke, "that *might* be a tough choice."

Michael didn't laugh.

A heavy silence settled in. Michael's eyes smoldered as he glared at the coffee table, silently telling himself the story of a life so bad that no one could blame him for choosing hell over his father.

Albert for his part was deep in silent prayer. He had pushed too hard and too far and had offended the Spirit. He could tell by the way he had suddenly buried himself in glib comebacks. When this happened, he loved his knowledge more than he loved Michael, his sin wickedly cloaked in the robes of piety. His soul ached. *Forgive me, Father,* he cried within. *Please, please, strip me of my pride. Please take it from me, Father. Please help me to desire the path of the low valley and the plain road.*[102] *Help me to love him, Father—to love him more than knowledge, to cherish him more than life. Please, dear Father. Forgive my broken soul. Please give me the words to say that might undo what I have done. Please open Michael's heart. Please bless me with thy Spirit, dear Lord, that I might not offend his spirit anymore.* He yearned for reconciliation and prayed for words that might help.

"I owe you an apology, Michael," he said quietly, not knowing what he was going to say.[103] "I've been inconsiderate of you."

Michael raised his head.

"You see, I've been to such a faraway country spiritually

that sometimes I assume I know everything about the bumps and bruises of life. And that's just arrogant. I don't know your situation—or your father's, for that matter. No heartache will be soothed by one who merely spouts doctrine at another's pain, even if the doctrine is true.[104] I'm sorry, my boy. Somewhere between yesterday and today I made myself into your teacher. And our conversation has been the poorer for it. Whatever does and doesn't happen between you and your father is between the two of you and the Lord. Look to the Spirit as your teacher, not to me. I apologize that I tried to step where I shouldn't have stepped. I hope you can forgive me."

Michael's shoulders went slack, and he dropped his chin to his chest. He bit his lower lip in an attempt to keep at bay the emotion he felt rising within. He no sooner had noticed this than the tears were rolling down his cheeks. His chest now was rising and falling in deep, heaving rolls. Between shudders he tried to respond. "No," he said, shaking his head, "no, Al," he sputtered. "You've done nothing wrong." He shook his head again. "Nothing." He wiped at his face. "Nothing wrong."

"Oh, but I have," Albert said. "I am sorry."

Michael shook his head more vigorously. "No," he said, beginning to get control over his breathing and his voice. "I'm the one with the problem." He took a deep breath, but the shudders suddenly came again halfway through. "I don't want to go to hell," he shook his head. "I don't want to be lost."

"I know Michael," Albert said. He came over and sat next to him. "I know."

And he really did know. During those long months of estrangement, he many times told himself the same thing: *Eternal marriage!* he had scoffed. *Only a fool would want to spend an eternity with Helen. If that's what the celestial kingdom requires, no thank you!* It was his own version of choosing hell over the hand he felt he had been unfairly dealt. But it was a lie, always a lie—a lie that threw responsibility for his own sins at another's feet. Looking back, the lie was obvious, of course. He wouldn't have had to make the point so forcefully to himself had it been true.

"You're right, Al," Michael said, wiping at his cheek. "You've been right all evening. I'm broken. Completely and utterly broken." He wiped at his tears again. "I'm a mess."

Albert looked at Michael. "I don't want to step where I shouldn't again," he said, "but would you mind if we read another scripture?"

Michael shook his head and rubbed his eyes. "Of course not. Please."

Albert opened the Bible to Matthew, chapter 11. He handed the book to Michael. "Take a look at verses 28 and 29," he said, "verses that immediately precede a discussion of the Sabbath."[105]

Michael cleared his throat and began to read.

> Come unto me, all ye that labour and are heavy
> laden, and I will give you rest. Take my yoke upon you,

and learn of me; for I am meek and lowly in heart: and
ye shall find rest unto your souls.[106]

Michael reread the verses again, the years of estrangement
from his father racing through his mind. He looked back up at
Albert. "I see. So you're saying that my heart has not been at
rest while it has been laboring toward my father." Michael nodded at the thought. "You're right, Al. You're absolutely right."

"I didn't say that," Albert replied.

"Well, you should have. It's true."

Michael closed his eyes and imagined a scene. He imagined
by the grace of God that he was admitted into the celestial kingdom. He was standing in a room of exquisite yet inviting brightness. The people around him stood in groups of two or more
each. They were engaged in serene and happy conversation.
Michael stood apart. He then imagined that his father walked
in, his body fully restored, his clothing white like the others. In
Michael's mind's eye, he imagined his father entering with a
couple of halting steps, his eyes filled with wonder and adjust-
ing to the light. The halting gait reminded Michael of his
father's drunkenness. At that thought, the vision began to dim.
His father turned to glance at him, but Michael quickly averted
his eyes. When he did, a veil of darkness immediately fell over
him and extinguished the scene. His father, the others, the tran-
quil brilliance of the room—all were instantly gone. Michael
bowed his head. "I'm in trouble," he whispered. "Deep
trouble."

"And how fortunate you are that you see that," Albert said, echoing the words Henry had spoken to him years earlier. "The question is, will you continue to insist on laboring to carry your own heavy burden, or will you take up the Savior's lighter burden and find rest to your soul?"

Michael looked up. "I want his rest," he said.

"Then let me share with you the sign of contrition you asked about." He handed Michael the Book of Mormon, opened again to 3 Nephi, chapter 12. "Go ahead and read verses 23 and 24. It's a passage we touched on yesterday."

Michael bowed his head and read.

> Therefore, if ye shall come unto me, or shall desire to come unto me, and rememberest that thy brother hath aught against thee—Go thy way unto thy brother, and first be reconciled to thy brother, and then come unto me with full purpose of heart, and I will receive you.[107]

Michael set the book down on his lap. He drew in a deep breath and looked up at Albert. "So I need to go see him," he said.

"That might be a start," Albert nodded.

"Then what else?"

"Why did the elder son in the parable resent his brother?" Albert asked.

"Because he thought he was better than his young brother," Michael answered.

"Do you think you're better than your father, Michael?"

Michael looked back down. Of course he thought this. How could he not?

"Think of Adam and Eve again," Albert said. "How many transgressions did it take for them to become separated from God?"

Michael cleared his throat. "One."

"What if they had committed twenty transgressions? Would they have been more separated?"

Michael thought about it. "No. Separated is separated."

"It follows from this, doesn't it," Albert asked, "that to commit only one transgression of the law is to suffer the whole effect of the law—separation from God? If we fail to keep the law in one respect, then we are, as it were, 'guilty of all,' and, as King Benjamin's people discovered, 'even less than the dust of the earth.'[108] After all, as Mormon noted, the dust exhibits what we do not: total obedience to the commandments of the Creator.[109] The sense that one is not even above the dust of the earth is the birth of a contrite spirit. And it would never occur to such a person to think, 'Yes, but I'm a better speck of dust than you are.'"

Michael laughed at the thought.

"The thought itself would be absurd, wouldn't it?" Albert said. "'Where is boasting then?' the Apostle Paul asked. His blunt answer was, 'It is excluded.'[110] As all are guilty under the law—guilty, in fact, of the entire effect of the law, which is separation from God—the law 'stops every mouth.'[111] It is simply hard and resentment-filled labor to maintain the fiction that I am more loved before the Lord than another, whatever the other may or may not have done. It is a prideful and accusing belief that will forever keep me barred from our Father's house. Take up instead, he invites us, his yoke of meekness and lowliness of heart—the realization that I deserve no better than another. Do so and I discover the rest I have long sought in all the wrong thoughts and opinions."

Albert looked at Michael and smiled. "The day the prodigal finally turned toward home was a Sabbath to him, as was the day the people of King Benjamin discovered they were beggars.[112] On those holy days, hearts turned toward those they had been callously resisting—hearts of children to fathers and fathers to children. Families in their tents bowed humbly and equally together. A downtrodden son found himself swept up into loving arms.

"That, my boy, is the sign of our turning. When we contritely recognize the damning reality of our own brokenness, no one else's brokenness can keep us from loving them, and we discover rest where all had been heartache. Your father, an elder son himself, may not receive you well at his bedside. That will be his choice to make. But will you receive him nonetheless, Michael? That is the question holiness asks. Will your heart turn to your father, so that your father's heart may be invited to turn toward you?"

"It sounds like you're speaking now of the temple," Michael said quietly.

"The work of holiness is a single work. All who contritely turn to their Father and make the humble walk home will one day be clothed in robes in his house. Holy days lead us to holy places, and holy places then transform our days. That is the order of things. It is the way we become prepared for his glory. "All those who 'keep my sabbaths,' the Lord told Isaiah, 'and choose the things that please me, and take hold of my covenant, even unto them will I [bring to my holy mountain and] give in mine house . . . a place and a name better than of sons and of daughters: I will give them an everlasting name, that shall not be cut off.'"[113]

"So the temple is connected to what we've been discussing tonight?" The thought renewed Michael's interest in the Lord's house.

"Every whit."

"How?"

Albert looked at the clock on the mantel. "I'm afraid that will have to be a discussion for another time."

Michael bowed his head again.

"But you can begin your own study of it now," Albert said.

"You're right," Michael nodded. "It's time I started going again."

"Then may I suggest a stop on the way?"

Michael looked up. "Hackensack?"

Albert nodded. "The work of the Sabbath is not limited to Sundays, Michael, nor is temple work limited to temples. If you commence the work of the Sabbath in regard to your father, his bedside will become a place of holiness to you—a place to prepare you for other places."

Michael looked at Albert in silence and then bowed his head again. He knew what he needed to do; he just wasn't sure he could do it.

17

THE BEGINNING OF REST

It was nearly midnight by the time Michael arrived home. He had expected to sleep heavily. Instead, he tossed and turned all night. His father's face and Albert's invitation kept coming to his mind. By 6:00 A.M. he was up and getting ready to drive to his sister Mary's place in Hackensack.

For reasons Michael couldn't fully explain, he was now feeling regret. His mother had died when Michael was just a child. His father, miserable in two later marriages, found company in the bottle. Father and son had barely spoken in ten years. As he scanned their history of silence, Michael could sense that he had let his father drown in loneliness over those years.

Loneliness! he shot back in defense. *Where do you think I learned it? From the man who never cared a lick about me! Or anyone else, for that matter! I would rather that he ridiculed my religion like my sister and brother did than that he yawned at that and every other choice I made.*

Angie's words from the prior Friday came to his mind again, *That's not fair.*

In her presence, Michael hadn't allowed himself to consider the truth in her comment, but her words echoed within him in the solitary hours of the morning. *Maybe detachment was the way Dad dealt with his loss,* he reasoned, *or with his pain.* And then, thinking about the anguish he himself sometimes felt even in a relatively healthy marriage, Michael wondered how difficult it must have been to suffer through two disastrous ones.

He caught himself. *But there I am again, letting him off the hook.*

This thought pulled him back into the conversation with Albert the night before. We are all on the hook, it turned out, not just his father. This realization mellowed his anger. While alcohol had never beckoned to Michael, Albert had awakened him to other things that pulled his mind and heart away from what was holy—his casualness, his anger, his resentment, his covetousness.

All that is ungodly within us must be put to death, Albert had said, *or we will not be able to enter into the presence of the Lord. He that is not purified shall not abide the day.*[114] The thought filled Michael with fear.

He and his father needed the same help, and although

Michael was still loaded with questions, he had more answers than ever about how that help could be delivered. He had a father who needed him now and in the future, and a long deceased mother who needed the same.

Realizing that the bitterness that had consumed him was itself an impurity from which he needed rescue, it suddenly occurred to Michael that he needed his father as much as his father needed him. For each, their spiritual wounds both resembled and involved the other. He rushed out to his car for the hour or so drive to Hackensack.

He prayed that his father would be coherent enough to hear him.

PART III

LOVING THE HOLY TEMPLE

18

SACRED SPACE

The alarm clock sounded at 6:00 A.M. Michael's hand pawed groggily around the top of the bed stand in search of the offending instrument. After nearly bumping it over the edge, he tapped the snooze button. He turned and looked up at the ceiling, groping for consciousness. *What day is it?* The absurd contradictions of his dreams still played with his senses. He squinted in an effort to focus both his eyes and his mind. *Why the alarm? Where am I supposed to be?*

The fog slowly began to lift. He remembered it was Saturday. His father had passed away the day before, and Albert would be over that morning at around 8:00 A.M. Despite his father's passing, Michael had insisted, over Albert's protestations, that they meet. If so, Albert said, he didn't want Michael to have to leave his home. He had insisted that they meet, if at all, at Michael's place rather than his own.

Michael had given himself an extra hour to pick up the place a bit, both for Albert and for Angie, who would be returning that evening. The next day would bring another trip to Hackensack, where Michael and his sister and brother would plan the Tuesday funeral service.

Michael pushed the sheet off and rolled his legs over the side of the bed. He slowly pulled himself up to a sitting position.

The events of the week cascaded through his mind. He had arrived at his sister's house on Tuesday just in time to help her and two nurses transfer his father to a new hospital bed. As he had helped lift him and observed him hanging in the hoist, it struck Michael how frail his father had become. He groaned in pain at every move they made and didn't even have the strength to hold up his own head. He was, in almost every respect, as vulnerable as a newborn baby.

The scene of vulnerability humanized him for Michael, and he could feel some of the deeply embedded barbs of resentment begin to break free. He spent most of the rest of that day in his father's room.

Michael's mind was also on Albert that day, since it was Albert's mention of temple-related work in Hackensack that had nudged Michael to his father's bedside. He had called Albert from his sister's home to thank him. Albert responded by personally delivering a week's worth of food and other supplies. He didn't want any of the family members to have to worry about anything as mundane as shopping.

As the evening grew late on Tuesday, Michael felt the desire to have a conversation with his father. For his father's part, this was difficult, of course, as his condition made it hard to speak. He could listen, however, and Michael could listen to his listening. Not wanting to burden his father further, he decided to say only the thoughts he felt prompted by the Spirit to speak, trusting that the Lord would give him to say what would be best for both of them. The result was the beginning of an apology, one Michael believed he must spend the rest of his own life finishing.

Michael had stayed the night on Tuesday, sleeping on his sister's couch. Over the next two days, he and his father were able to spend some important moments together. However, by Thursday it was evident that his father wouldn't live more than another day or two. The family gathered. Joining Michael and his sister and brother were five of his father's siblings, one of his mother's sisters, two great-uncles, and a great-aunt.

Michael had disliked some of these people nearly as much as his father. Abuse, gluttony, and bigotry flowed freely in the family's blood, and Michael had been more than happy to keep his distance over the years. This crew took up residence around the bedside and began to reminisce. At first, the sight was too oddly incongruous for Michael to take seriously. One uncle had swindled another out of tens of thousands of dollars, for example, yet here they were standing next to each other telling stories. Two of the aunts had been married to the same man— the first blaming the second for the failure of her marriage— and yet they, too, stood smiling. After awhile, Michael forgot his critique of the family and joined with them.

In the evening, a minister assigned by hospice joined the family at the bedside. They held hands and sang about the Savior, and the minister offered a prayer. Over the hours that followed, all the members of the family had a chance to spend a few private moments with him.

Before leaving his father that final time, Michael leaned over the bed, putting a hand on either side of his father's head. He bent down close and whispered that he loved him. Michael was almost startled to hear himself say the words; he had neither felt nor uttered them in years. The moment was unplanned and unrehearsed, his desire to pull himself close spontaneous, the words just there for him.

His father's eyes remained closed, but a faint smile tugged at the corners of his mouth. As Michael pushed himself up and turned to leave, his father's fingers moved to touch Michael's right hand. Michael grabbed back at the fingers and collapsed into the chair next to the bed, sobbing.

His father was gone by the next morning.

As Michael now prepared the house for Albert's arrival, he was grateful to be anticipating company. He looked forward as well to continuing his sessions with Albert. "Sessions" sounded so clinical—almost like he was meeting Albert for therapy. *Maybe I am,* he laughed.

There was a soft knocking on the door at precisely 8:00 A.M.

"Hello, Michael," Albert exclaimed when Michael opened the door. Under his left arm was a box filled with bagels and cream cheese. He carried a gallon of orange juice in his right. "I thought you could use something to eat."

"Thanks, Albert. That's really thoughtful of you. Please, come in." He invited Albert into the living room.

"It's okay to eat in here?" Albert asked.

"It is until tonight," Michael laughed.

"Ah, living on the edge are you?" Albert joked as he sat down on the couch.

"It seriously would be the edge if Angie were here. Since she's still in Seattle, I'd say I'm living somewhere in the middle of the plateau."

"Very well," Albert said. "But be sure to vacuum the plateau before tonight," he winked, "or it will have been the edge."

Michael laughed. He sat down in the chair across from Albert, and Albert passed the bagels to him. "How'd it turn out with your family?" Albert asked.

The question brought the week and its emotions streaming back. Michael fought to keep his composure. "It was—" he began, intending to share the miracle of his time with his father. He opened his mouth to continue but could not squeeze any sound through the knot in his throat. He gulped in the futile attempt to release the emotional pressure and keep the tears at bay.

"I'm sorry, Albert," he choked. He wiped at his cheek.

"No need to be sorry, my boy. Tears can come unexpectedly at times. I know what that's like."

Michael nodded.

"Besides," Albert continued, "the tears are a blessing."

Michael looked up at him through reddened eyes.

"It means that you loved him. Despite it all, despite all that did and didn't happen between you over the years, you came to love him."

Michael remembered the final evening with his father, when the tears wouldn't stop flowing. The fingers that had weakly reached out to touch Michael's resolutely returned his grip for as long as Michael remained by him. *Yes, it had ended—unexpectedly, even unfathomably—in love.*

Michael cleared his throat. "You started talking about the temple on Monday," he said with renewed interest in light of his father's passing. "I'm wondering if we could pick up our conversation from there."

"Maybe we should talk about it some other time, Michael."

"Why not now?"

"With all you've been through this week?"

"*Because* of what I've been through," Michael replied. "I shudder to think what this week would have been like had I not started it in conversation with you, Albert. Nothing is more important to me, and perhaps to my father as well, than continuing that conversation. Please," he said.

Albert exhaled in resignation. "Okay, but on one condition."

"Anything."

"You tell me the moment you are beginning to get weary."

Michael shrugged. His time earlier in the week with Albert had been invigorating, and he anticipated more of the same. "If I start to wear down, I'll let you know. I promise."

Albert looked at the scriptures Michael had placed on the table between them. "Looks like you're prepared."

"I figured we'd be needing them," Michael smiled.

"Very well, then. Let me start with a question: What has kept you from the temple?"

19

A GRACIOUS DEAL

Michael shook his head. "I don't know," he said. "I don't think it's been anything in particular. It just hasn't connected for me somehow. I feel like I'm missing something. Or," he added, "that the temple is missing something." He bit his lower lip, unsure whether he should have mentioned his last thought. "Oh, there *is* one thing," he added, partly in order to divert attention. "I don't understand the formalism. Why such legalistic ordinances, for example? I don't understand why the Lord would need to use them. If the point is having our hearts sanctified and made pure, as you suggested Monday, then I don't see where such rigid formalism is necessary. Just let the Holy Ghost do his sanctifying work. Why do we need more than that?"

"An interesting objection for one who spends his days working on contracts."

"I know. It seems strange that I would have a problem with legalism. It's just that while I understand why we need contracts in the world, I'm not sure why the *Lord* needs them."

"The Lord *doesn't* need them, Michael."

"Then why does he require us to enter into them?"

"I would think that answer would be obvious," Albert responded. "He requires it because *we* need them."

"Why?"

Albert sat in silence for a moment. "Do you know of a board game called *The Settlers of Catan?*" he finally said.

"I think I've heard of it. Never played it, though."

"It's a pretty fun game, actually," Albert said.

"Who do you play it with?" Michael asked. He instantly regretted the question, as it pointed to Albert's loneliness.

"I have a grandnephew who loves the game," he said. "I bought a copy so we can play when he comes over."

Michael nodded. "And the game has something to do with the temple?" he asked.

"No," Albert chuckled, "it's not as good as that. But it has illuminated an important gospel point for me—a point about our need for heavenly contracts. That's what I want to mention to you." After a brief pause he plunged onward. "The game has five resources you accumulate and then trade to build cities. The resources are wood, brick, ore, wheat, and lamb. There is a strategy involved in accumulating them, of course, and during one particular game with my grandnephew, Jacob, I bungled my strategy and ended up being shut out of lamb. Jacob had a corner on it. Which meant, of course, that I was done. There was no way for me to win, except one: I needed a deal; I needed Jacob to trade some lamb to me."

"Why would he do that?" Michael laughed.

"Exactly," Albert said. "I got myself into my own predicament. On my own merits, all was lost. Game over.

"But Jacob offered me a deal anyway. Even though by the rules of the game I was finished and deserved nothing but to lose, and even though I had nothing that he needed, he traded me some lamb. He offered me a way to stay in the game."

"Nice kid."

"He's a great boy, actually, yes."

"But I bet he stuck it to you in the deal, didn't he—one or two lamb for tons of everything else, for example?"

Albert shook his head. "Two lamb for two wood."

"Wow, that's a really nice kid!"

"He was merciful to me, to be sure. It was an act of grace, a gift. A gift," he continued, "that is analogous to the Lord's gift to us, Michael. Think about it. Without a deal, we are lost forever. We have no claim to a deal—we have failed on our own accord, have nothing to offer that the Lord needs, and are condemned under the laws of justice. We deserve the spiritual death we talked about on Monday. Yet still, the Lord offered us a deal—or, in scriptural language, a covenant. This is what is meant when the scriptures say that he is the 'author' of our faith.[115] He authored—or created—a way for us to stay in the game, as it were. And like Jacob's offering, it was a pure act of mercy and grace. Furthermore, his grace did not end at the offering of a deal. Like Jacob, the Lord offers us merciful terms—terms we can comply with, terms we don't deserve. This, too, is part of his mercy and grace.

"Here, however, Jacob's mercy stopped far short of the Lord's. You see, part of the Lord's grace, as we talked about on Monday, is that he offers us his Spirit, which tells us 'all things what we should do.'[116] It is as if Jacob, after giving me the lamb, would have guided me in all my future moves in the game, whispering instructions that would have led me to victory. He didn't do this, of course, but that is precisely what the Lord offers us. If we comply with the merciful terms of his deal or covenant, he will walk with and guide us.

"Yet his grace goes even further than this. For notwithstanding the grace of the deal, the grace of its terms, and the grace of the Spirit that invites us to comply with those terms, each of us fails to live up to the terms of the covenant. We condemn ourselves once again. This happened in my game with Jacob. It turns out that I made a foolish move and squandered the lamb he had graciously given me. Had I made a different play with the lamb, I probably would have won the game, but I made a mistake. I recognized the mistake almost the moment I made it, but it was too late. I had squandered my last lamb. Again, I had no hope unless Jacob would forgive my mistake and offer me lamb once again."

"Did he?" Michael asked.

Albert laughed. "No. This time he crushed me. But the Lord doesn't. He offers us the grace of repentance.[117] We are 'saved by grace after all we can do,' the scriptures say, which is why the Savior is not only the 'author' of our faith but also its 'finisher.'[118] However, the king of the Anti-Nephi-Lehies taught his people that 'all we can do' is to repent![119] When we repent of our failure to comply with the gracious terms of the covenant, the Lord allows us to 'stay in the game,' as it were. He is able and willing to offer us this repentance because he graciously took upon himself the crushing weight of our sinfulness, so that both the stain of, and the desire for, sin might be 'taken away from our hearts.'"[120]

Michael's mind was racing. The story of Albert's predicament with his nephew, Jacob, and Jacob's subsequent gracious offering, captured man's total dependence on the Lord in a way Michael had never seen. *I'm only in the game because of the grace of the Lord's covenant,* he realized. *And then to think that even though the Lord could have required any terms he wanted, he offered us terms we can keep, including the incredibly merciful condition of repentance, a condition that itself was enabled only because of the grace of his suffering.* These thoughts captured Michael's imagination.

"Do you remember on Monday how we looked at two separate questions—how the Lord has power to change our broken hearts, and what we need to do to allow him to change us?"

Michael nodded.

"In answer to the first question, I shared the analogy of a king's offering to save his people, remember?"

"Of course. I loved it."

"In answer to the second question," Albert continued, "we discussed how the commandments are designed to bring us to our knees in contrition before the Lord. Only then, when we ourselves come with full purpose of heart to the Lord, thinking ourselves no better than others, can the Lord replace our broken hearts with his own."

Michael nodded. "I remember."

"Then think of the analogy of the game I just described. Likewise, when I came to Jacob in need of lamb, he graciously gave me the lamb I needed. But I only came to him because the game had terms I had failed to keep. Had there been no terms under which I was condemned, I would have felt no need to go to Jacob for a deal."

"Right, that's the point about the commandments that you talked about on Monday. They awaken us to our sins and therefore to our need for Christ. I get that."

"Actually, Michael, you've left one part out. A critical part too, since it's where the temple fits in the picture."

"Really?" Michael asked hopefully. "What have I missed?"

"Two things, actually. Here's the first. Since it's precisely my will or desire that must be sanctified and made holy in order to be able to abide the glory of God, the Lord cannot change me *against* my will. I must, as Elder Neal A. Maxwell taught, lay my will on the altar before the Lord through a sacrifice of a broken heart and a contrite spirit."[121]

"Yes, I understand that," Michael said.

"Do you?"

Albert's reply made Michael less sure. "I think so."

"This is not a single offering," Albert replied. "I'm not suggesting I need approach the Lord in contrition only once and that he will then change the whole of me. Far from it. Agency demands that I am freely consenting to the changes the Lord stands willing to make in me. To sacrifice is to know what it is I am willing to give up. If the Lord were to surprise me and change what I didn't know I was asking him to change, he would be changing parts of me without my consent. He would be usurping my will, which, since his work is precisely to invite us through our own volition to allow him to *change* our wills, is something he cannot do."

Michael was still searching for where Albert was going. He sensed something important, but he could only barely see the outlines of the point through the mist that still obscured his view.

"It follows, then," Albert said, "that we need to know every piece of us that needs, as it were, more Lamb. We need to see every weakness, every fault, every failing, every transgression— which, as we have discussed, is exactly what the gospel can show us. Brigham Young said that 'the gospel . . . causes men and women to reveal that which would have slept in their dispositions until they dropped into their graves. The plan by which the Lord leads his people makes them reveal their thoughts and intents, and brings out every trait of disposition lurking in their [beings].'[122] 'Come unto me,' the Savior said, and 'I will show unto [men] their weakness. . . . If they humble themselves before me, and have faith in me, then will I make weak things become strong unto them.'[123] So if we go to the Lord contritely, in faith, laying each of these transgressions and faults on the altar before him, he will consume them through the power of the Holy Ghost. But again, we know what needs to be consumed on the altar only if we understand what is required of us under the covenant."

A shaft of light started to cut through the confusion in Michael's mind. "I see. You're saying the Lord can't just change us generally because to do so would be to override the will he is trying to sanctify in us. We need to know every term or requirement in the covenant the Lord has extended to us so that we can know when we need to come to him for rescue from every violation of those terms. We need to have our hearts changed term by term so that in the end there is no part of us that still desires sin. So the terms or requirements of the deal matter; that's what you're saying. We have to know what they are."

Albert smiled. "That is what I believe. Which leads to the second issue: What is the best way to invite mankind to learn the terms of the covenant?"

After a moment's thought, Michael shrugged. "I'm not sure."

"Well," Albert said, "in your line of work, how do you ensure that your clients understand the terms of the agreements they are entering into?"

"Well, personally, I review the terms with my clients, item by item."

"You teach them, then, line upon line, precept upon precept, as the Lord does."[124]

Michael smiled at the way Albert so easily made connection with the scriptures. "I suppose so, yes."

"And is there anything that drives your teaching and their learning?" Albert asked. "Is there anything that speeds that process up and helps them and you to focus?"

Michael thought about the almost endless "closings" he had been part of during his career. "Closing" is the word used to describe the final act whereby individuals or corporations enter into agreements. For example, when purchasing a home, the buyers sit and sign all of the financing, title, and other documents necessary to consummate the deal. This is a closing. In very large business deals, the looming closing date typically drives the final negotiations. Michael had participated in many of these "final pushes," and in response to Albert's question he pictured some of these events: people were finally huddled in a room together, reaching agreement on matters that might have been left hanging forever had they not been pushed by the closing date. "Sure," he answered. "Since the parties have to understand the terms of any agreement before they sign it, the act of signing an agreement itself drives the participants' preparation and learning. In the law, we call these signing ceremonies *closings*."

"In the gospel," Albert said, "we call these signing ceremonies *ordinances*."

20

PREPARING FOR HEAVENLY BRIGHTNESS

Michael rocked backward in his seat.

Of course, he thought to himself. *The Lord's not binding himself to some legalistic formality by requiring that all mankind receive the necessary ordinances. He's simply making the execution step plain for us, and by so doing inviting us to learn and commit ourselves to the terms of the covenant.* Michael smiled in wonder. *How could I have been so blind?* "So you're talking about all the ordinances of the gospel, Al?"

"All of the saving ordinances, yes," Albert answered, "beginning with baptism. Each saving ordinance signals the acceptance of certain terms of the Lord's gracious oath and covenant."

"Oath and covenant?" Michael asked. The terms had leaped

out at him, straight from the pages of the eighty-fourth section of the Doctrine and Covenants. "As in the oath and covenant of the priesthood?"

"The oath and covenant of the priesthood is a vital part of the Lord's overall covenant with us," Albert nodded. "This grand, overall covenant is sometimes called 'the new and everlasting covenant,' which, the scriptures reveal, was 'instituted for the fulness of [God's] glory'—that is, in order to prepare man to withstand the fulness of God's glory. No one who rejects this covenant, the scriptures say, 'can be permitted to enter [his] glory.'[125]

"The Lord's oath and covenant to us," Albert continued, "is that so long as we offer every unholy piece of ourselves to him to be changed, he will sanctify us by the Spirit and renew and seal up our bodies in glory so that we can abide the glory of God.[126] If we do this, the power that seals us up unto the glory of God will protect and seal not only our bodies but also our holy agreements and associations, extending these, as well, beyond the grave.[127] That is his gracious deal—his oath and covenant—to us,[128] an oath and covenant that culminates in the forgotten ordinances of the temple."

"The forgotten ordinances?" Michael asked.

"Yes."

"I'm not sure I understand."

"The crowning ordinances of the Lord's covenant had been lost from the earth and had to be restored. This was the angel

Moroni's message when he appeared to Joseph Smith. Moroni quoted Malachi to the effect that a messenger would come 'before . . . the great and dreadful day of the Lord'—the day when the Lord would come in glory—to restore priesthood authority that had been lost from Israel since the time of Moses."[129]

"Elijah," Michael said.

"That's right," Albert nodded. "Elijah's return, in accordance with Malachi's prophecy, occurred on April 3, 1836.[130] He appeared to Joseph Smith and Oliver Cowdery as they knelt in prayer in the Kirtland Temple.[131] He restored to the earth the keys of the crowning ordinances of the holy priesthood—the forgotten ordinances of the temple. These were the ordinances the Lord was talking about when Malachi quoted him as saying, 'Even from the days of your fathers ye are gone away from mine ordinances, and have not kept them.'[132] He then pointed to the purpose for those ordinances in his next sentence: 'Return unto me, and I will return unto you, saith the Lord of hosts.'[133] In other words, the Lord was saying, 'When you return to the ordinances of the temple, I will be able to return to you.'"

"So it's through the ordinances of the temple that we are prepared to be admitted into the presence of God?" Michael asked.

"That is what I understand the scriptures to say."

"Where?"

"Well, Malachi just alluded to it," Albert said, "but let's look at a more direct reference." He motioned for Michael to join him on the couch. "Let's take a look at this together." Michael came and sat next to him, and Albert set the scriptures on the table before them.

"The clearest explanation I know for how the ordinances of the temple prepare us for the glory of God is contained in the eighty-fourth section of the Doctrine and Covenants."

"The oath and covenant of the priesthood," Michael said.

"Exactly," Albert nodded. "The passage we normally refer to as the oath and covenant spans verses 33 through 40 of section 84. However, in order to understand those verses, we need to look at them in context." Albert pointed at verse 5. "The section begins with a prophecy that the Lord will come in glory to the temple in the last days." He then turned the page and pointed at verse 32. "Twenty-seven verses later, beginning in the verse immediately preceding what is normally considered the start of the oath and covenant, the Lord returns to the theme and says that the bodies of the sons of Moses and of Aaron— the priesthood holders—will be renewed and sanctified so that they will be able to be filled with the Lord's glory when he comes."[134]

"So what are the twenty-seven verses in between about?" Michael asked.

"Good question. Another way to state it would be to ask this: 'What do we need to know in order for us to understand how people can be sanctified and renewed so that they can abide the glory of God?'"

Michael nodded. "Okay, then, what do we need to know?"

"Let's take a look." Albert pointed at verse 19. "Let's start here, where we are taught some important information about the holy priesthood."

And this greater [or Melchizedek] priesthood administereth the gospel and holdeth the key . . . of the knowledge [or presence[135]] of God. Therefore in the ordinances thereof, the power of godliness is manifest. And without the ordinances thereof, and the authority of the priesthood, the power of godliness is not manifest unto men in the flesh; for without this no man can see the face of God, even the Father, and live.

Now this Moses plainly taught to the children of Israel in the wilderness, and sought diligently to sanctify his people that they might behold the face of God; but they hardened their hearts and could not endure his presence; therefore, the Lord . . . swore that they should not enter into his rest while in the wilderness, which rest is the fulness of his glory. Therefore, he took Moses out of their midst, and the Holy Priesthood also.[136]

"There's a lot there," Michael said.

"Let's unpack it, shall we?"

"Please."

"Let's start toward the end of the passage. What does it say Moses was trying to prepare his people for?"

Michael looked back down at the verses. After rereading them, he replied, "It says he was trying to sanctify his people so that they could see the face of God and enter into the fulness of his glory. A pretty grandiose plan, I might add."

"Actually, that was the plan of all the patriarchs from the beginning," Albert responded. "Enoch's people had, after all, been taken up into heaven on account of their sanctification and holiness.[137] The scriptures suggest that Melchizedek and his people may have been taken up into the presence of God in like manner.[138] And the Prophet Joseph taught that Abraham, too, sought to bring his posterity into the presence of God.[139]

"Moses, like Enoch, Melchizedek, and Abraham before him, was seeking to 'obtain heaven' with his people.[140] This meant, as we have discussed, that they had to become sanctified—made pure as the Lord is pure—so that they could endure the Lord's presence."

Michael nodded.

"And, as we have discussed," Albert continued, "the Lord appointed a way for the sanctification of his people. It was to take place through the Lord's new and everlasting covenant—the covenant through which man is 'permitted to enter into [God's] glory.'[141] 'Every fault that a person has will be made manifest [by the gospel],' Brigham Young taught, 'that it may be corrected by the Gospel of salvation, by the laws of the Holy Priesthood.'[142] Our acceptance of each of the covenant's terms was to be marked by our receiving the connected ordinances of the holy priesthood, the crowning ordinances of which are administered by that priesthood in the place the Lord instructed Moses how to build: the temple.[143] *All this* is what Moses plainly taught his people in the wilderness. With that bit of background, listen again to verses 19 through 22."

And this greater priesthood administereth the gospel and holdeth the key of the mysteries of the kingdom, even the key of the knowledge [or presence[144]] of God. Therefore, in the ordinances thereof, the power of godliness is manifest. And without the ordinances thereof, and the authority of the priesthood, the power of godliness is not manifest unto men in the flesh; for without this no man can see the face of God, even the Father, and live.[145]

Michael suddenly thought of an objection to what he thought he was hearing. "So we can't see the face of God the Father and live unless we receive the ordinances of the temple?"

"That's what this passage seems to say," Albert nodded. "It says that the power of godliness, which one needs in order to behold the face of God, cannot be manifest to us in the flesh without the ordinances of the holy priesthood, a point that is taught symbolically in the temple as well."[146]

"But that can't be true," Michael objected. "It can't be the case that men have to receive the ordinances of the priesthood in order to see the face of God."

"Why do you say that?" Albert questioned him.

"Well, isn't it obvious? Many people have seen God over the ages without having received them."

"Like who?"

"Like Joseph Smith, for example, and Moses."

"Two great examples," Albert agreed.

"And they don't trouble you?" Michael asked.

"Trouble me?" Albert repeated. "On the contrary, they make my heart sing."

"But don't they disprove your point?"

"Speaking of Moses," Albert responded, "Joseph Smith revealed that he did, in fact, receive the ordinances of the holy priesthood.[147] But that brings us to Joseph himself. You are right, of course, that he had not received the ordinances of the priesthood before seeing both the Son and the Father. So how can we account for that, given this passage of scripture?"

"That's what I'm asking," Michael said.

"The answer is that while the ordinances of the holy priesthood are required to see a fulness of the glory of God—something all of us one day will need to be able to see if we want to dwell with him—they are not required in order to see merely a portion of that glory. The Father could choose to veil the fulness of his glory rather than shine forth his face in the 'fulness of the Father.'[148] But Moses was trying to prepare his people for a fulness.[149] When they hardened their hearts and refused to abide the law of a celestial glory, Moses, and the priesthood that was appointed to prepare them to receive a fulness, was removed from them.[150] The lesser priesthood remained, we are taught, 'which priesthood holds the key of the ministering of angels' but not the key of the presence of God, which is held by the greater priesthood.[151]

"The holy ordinances of the temple were forgotten."

21

PROMISES FOR ALL

With that context," Albert continued, "we can now move a few verses later to what has come to be called 'the oath and covenant of the priesthood.' I think you might hear it differently now."

> For whoso is faithful unto the obtaining these two priesthoods of which I have spoken, and the magnifying their calling, are sanctified by the Spirit unto the renewing of their bodies [so that they can be filled with the glory of the Lord], . . .
>
> And also all they who receive this priesthood receive me, saith the Lord; for he that receiveth my servants receiveth me; and he that receiveth me receiveth my Father; and he that receiveth my Father receiveth

ny Father's kingdom; therefore all that my Father hath shall be given unto him.

And this is according to the oath and covenant which belongeth to the priesthood. Therefore, all those who receive the priesthood, receive this oath and covenant of my Father, which he cannot break, neither can it be moved.[152]

Albert put the book down and turned to Michael. "What did you hear?"

Michael had heard a pattern. "The word *receive* repeats over and over."

"That's right. The passage begins with a statement regarding those who *obtain* the priesthood—that is, those who are ordained to the priesthood. After saying that those priesthood holders who magnify their callings will be sanctified and enabled to see God, the oath and covenant then transitions to a discussion regarding those who *receive* the priesthood. That transition begins with, 'And also all they who receive this priesthood receive me.'[153] Which raises this question: Are the phrases 'those who obtain the priesthood' and 'those who receive the priesthood' synonymous? Or, when the Lord says, 'And also all they who receive this priesthood,' is he making a transition to a group of people that is different from those who merely hold the priesthood?"

Michael considered the question and then shrugged. "I'm not sure."

"Let's think about it. We've already been taught in the preceding verses that priesthood holders who magnify their priesthood will be able to receive the glory of the Lord, right?"

Michael nodded.

"Well, let me ask you this, then. According to what we learn from the Moses story about the necessity of the ordinances of the holy priesthood if we hope to receive the glory of God, will priesthood holders who have not received the ordinances of the temple be able to receive that glory?"

Michael shook his head.

"So it would appear, then, that magnifying one's priesthood calling in this context includes receiving the ordinances of the temple."

After thinking about it, Michael said, "That seems right, yes."

Albert continued. "That is, they themselves have to *receive* the priesthood—the ordinances of the priesthood at the hands of other priesthood holders—in order to receive the Lord. Right?"

"Yes, I guess so," Michael said. And then he saw where Albert was going with this. "Oh, I get it. When the Lord said, 'And also all they who receive this priesthood receiveth me,' he is reiterating what we learned earlier: the ordinances of the holy priesthood that we receive from priesthood holders in the temple prepare us to receive the glory of God."

"I believe that's right, Michael. So will everyone who holds the priesthood be able to receive the glory of God?"

"No," Michael answered, "only those who have received the ordinances of the priesthood. And," he added, "who have magnified the priesthood that they hold."

"How about those who don't hold the priesthood?" Albert asked. "How about women, for example. Does this promise about being able to receive the glory of God apply to them as well?"

"It had better. Women need to be able to receive God's presence as much as men do."

"Of course," Albert agreed. "We learn in the temple that men and women are able to enter God's presence on identical terms. The ordinances of the holy priesthood clothe them in glory and prepare them for God's presence."

All of a sudden it made perfect sense to Michael. "So when the Lord says, 'And also all they who receive this priesthood receiveth me,' he is transitioning to a group that is in some ways broader and in some ways narrower than mere priesthood holders per se. Whether holders of the priesthood or not, we must receive the ordinances of the temple, and keep the covenants that correspond to them, in order to receive the presence of the Lord." Michael's voice trailed off. "So the oath and covenant of the priesthood applies as much to women as it does to men."

"The portions having to do with being able to receive the

presence of God do, yes," Albert replied. "As you said, they *must*, since *all of us*—men, women, all mankind—need to be sanctified for the coming of the glory of the Lord. Which is why," he added, "most of the rest of section 84 is about taking this knowledge and promise to the ends of the earth through missionary work. *And* why there will be much to do during the thousand years of preparation during the Millennium, a time of terrestrial glory,[14] to prepare mankind for the coming of the fulness of the glory of the Father—celestial glory."

Michael shook his head. "I can't believe I've never seen any of this before."

"Well, there's a lot to see," Albert nodded.

Michael turned to him. "How did you learn all this?"

"I've been around a long time." Then he smiled. "With no kids and no hobbies to speak of, I guess I've had an abundance of available time."

"Still—" Michael's voice trailed off.

"I'm just an old man who's trying to walk the path, Michael. Besides, nothing we've talked about is complicated. It's in plain sight in the scriptures."

"In sight maybe," Michael said. "I don't know about plain. I'm not sure how I'm going to remember all this."

"Just keep the big picture in mind, and the Spirit will guide you in any necessary details."

"That's just it. I'm not sure I can remember the big picture even."

"You might think about it this way," Albert said. "Do you deserve exaltation?"

Michael laughed resignedly. "No."

"Then you need a deal, don't you?"

Michael nodded.

"And what do you need in the deal?"

"I need to be changed—sanctified, so that I can enter again into the presence of God."

"Exactly. And what does the Lord need in the deal?"

"What does the *Lord* need?"

"Yes."

Michael thought about it. In the world, two parties enter into contract with each other only when each of them needs something from the other. If only one party is in need, the two parties never come together. But this contract wasn't like that at all. Only one party needed this deal—himself, or mortal man in general. Yet the Lord offered a deal anyway. It was a gift, an act of grace. The entire covenant was an act of grace.

"Nothing," Michael marveled.

"That is correct, Michael. You've heard the term, 'a covenant people'"?

Michael nodded halfheartedly, his mind still lost in his thoughts.

"The title is an admission of our complete and utter dependence on the Lord. We are people who needed a covenant—a 'deal.' Without a deal, all would have been lost. And so the

Lord granted us one—a merciful covenant we didn't and don't deserve, with gracious terms we can actually uphold, despite our deep imperfections, since our failure to fully live those terms is specifically accounted for under the covenant!

"And as you know from your legal work, of course, in order to receive the benefits of a covenant or deal, the parties must execute their acceptance of it."

Michael nodded.

"In your world, they do so by signing it. How do we do that with the Lord?"

"By receiving his ordinances," Michael answered.

"But why?" Albert asked. "Why must we formally witness our acceptance of the covenant in the first place? Since the Lord is so gracious, why doesn't he just accept us without it?"

This was precisely the question that had troubled Michael for years. But no more. "Because the terms matter," he said. "Each law of heaven we are struggling to live exposes the unholiness within us and shows us what we need to take to the Lord for sanctification. The Lord requires us to execute our acceptance of the terms of the covenant through the saving ordinances of the gospel in order to invite us to learn and to live the heavenly law."

"See, Michael?" Albert said. "You understand all this more than you think you do."

A hint of a smile tugged at the corners of Michael's mouth.

"I have another question, though," Albert said.

"Of course you do," Michael chuckled.

Albert grinned. "You said that the terms and therefore the ordinances of the covenant matter."

Michael nodded.

"Who else do you suppose they matter to?"

Michael looked blankly at Albert.

"They matter to your father."

22

RETHINKING
RESPONSIBILITY

If it's true that all mankind must know and take upon themselves each of the terms of the covenant so that they can know every whit of unholiness that must be taken from them, then it follows that all who have ever lived must receive the ordinances of the holy priesthood. Unless the hearts of the children turn to their fathers in such a way that allows this to happen even for those who have passed on, the angel Moroni declared to Joseph Smith, 'the whole earth would be utterly wasted at [the Lord's] coming,'[155] being unable to dwell with God."

"That's why we have proxy ordinances," Michael said.

"Yes, it is. But do you understand how it is that we are able to perform proxy ordinances, and why we are condemned if, despite our ability to do them, we don't?"

"Condemned?"

Albert nodded.

"Isn't that a little strong?"

Albert opened the Bible to the twenty-third chapter of Matthew. "Let me read you something," he said, "something that speaks to your question. It's a passage of scripture that has perplexed me for over a year now."

This intrigued Michael. "What passage?"

"Matthew 23 contains the strongest rebuke I know of in the scriptures," Albert replied. "It's the chapter where the Lord calls the scribes and the Pharisees 'whited sepulchres.'[156] Within a span of seven verses he calls them hypocrites four times, each time with exclamation.[157] Following the last of these, he says this:

> Woe unto you, scribes and Pharisees, hypocrites! because ye build the tombs of the prophets, and garnish the sepulchres of the righteous, and say, If we had been in the days of our fathers, we would not have been partakers with them in the blood of the prophets. . . .
>
> Wherefore, behold, I send unto you prophets, and wise men, and scribes: and some of them ye shall kill and crucify; and some of them shall ye scourge in your synagogues, and persecute them from city to city: that

upon you may come all the righteous blood shed upon the earth, from the blood of righteous Abel unto the blood of Zacharias son of Barachias, whom ye slew between the temple and the altar. . . .

Ye <u>bear testimony against your fathers, when ye,</u> <u>yourselves, are partakers of the same wickedness.</u> Behold your fathers did it through ignorance, but ye do not: wherefore, their sins shall be upon your heads."[158]

Albert looked up from the book. "Do you notice anything interesting in that?"

Michael's eyes opened wide at the question. "I wouldn't want the Lord talking to me like <u>that, that's for sure."</u>

"If the Lord's <u>words applied only to those</u> to whom he was speaking, the authors of the scriptures <u>likely wouldn't have</u> <u>bothered to record</u> them for us. So the question for us is what these words imply about us."

Michael sat up taller.

"Here's what I find stunning in these verses," Albert continued. "You've probably read a few scriptures where it says that <u>if the fathers fall into sin, the sins of the children shall be upon</u> <u>the heads of their fathers."[159]</u>

Michael nodded.

"The passage I've just read turns that around and says that, in the same way, the <u>sins of the fathers can be on the heads of</u> <u>the children."</u>

"It does?"

"Yes. The Savior here says that upon the scribes and the Pharisees would fall 'all the righteous blood shed upon the earth,' beginning with 'the blood of righteous Abel,' someone who died long before they came on the scene. It then goes on to say that the <u>sins of ignorant progenitors will be answerable on the heads of their willful descendants.</u>"

This violated everything Michael had been taught about personal responsibility. "That can't be right," he said. "My father, for example, made his own choices. I can't be responsible for what he himself chose."

Albert looked at Michael for a moment. "I'm going to ask you something that will seem to be a change of subject. It isn't, as you will see, but it might seem so at first."

"Okay," Michael consented.

"Something significant happened between you and your father this past week, didn't it?"

Michael nodded reverently. "Yes," he said. "Something beautiful, actually."

"Would you mind sharing any of it with me?" Albert asked. "Only if you're comfortable, of course. I don't want to intrude."

Michael felt himself transported back in memory to the long, cleansing Thursday-night sob at his father's bedside. "My father reached out to me on his final night. He couldn't speak, but he touched me with his finger. And when he did, something happened in me. It was like a dam burst or something. I just broke down crying." Michael shook his head as he remembered. "The tears seemed to wash away more than twenty years of bitterness and hate."

"And how is it that you were so close to your father that he was able to reach out and touch you?"

Michael relived the scene. "I was about to leave him for the final time when I stopped and leaned over him and whispered that I loved him." A tear cascaded down Michael's cheek.

"Ah," Albert nodded. "So in response to your offering to him, he reached out to you. And in response to his reaching out to you, you felt your heart reaching out to him."

Michael considered this. "Yes."

"Your offerings to each other helped each other to change."

After a moment's reflection, Michael replied, "Yes, I suppose they did."

"What if you had never made those offerings?"

Michael knew the answer to this. "Our estrangement would have continued," he said, "right through to his death."

"And beyond," Albert added.

"Yes," Michael nodded sadly, "probably so."

"Then I have a question for you: If you had chosen *not* to reach out to your father and things had ended bitterly, would you have had any responsibility for that bitterness?"

"For mine?" Michael asked, touching his chest.

"It's unquestionable you would have been responsible for your own bitterness," Albert replied. "Right?"

Michael nodded.

"Then how about your father's?"

Michael fought the notion. "He would have been responsible for his bitterness the same way I would have been responsible for mine," he answered.

"That sounds equitable," Albert nodded, "and true, as far as it goes. But what if responsibility goes further than that? What if, to the degree you didn't do your best to reach out to each other, you each would have been responsible both for your own and for the other's bitterness?"

"Are you saying that's the way it is, Al," Michael challenged, "or are you merely suggesting another possibility?"

Albert smiled at the joust. "Remember the story of the city of Sodom?"

"Sodom?" Michael wondered how it was relevant.

"The Lord agreed to save the entire city if merely ten righteous people could be found within its walls. That is, a mere ten souls coming repentantly to the Lord would have saved the whole."

"But none were found," Michael said.

"Exactly. So what is the level of the people's responsibility? Are they each responsible only for their own destruction? Or are they responsible as well for the destruction of others—destruction that would have been stayed had they themselves repented?"

Michael had no response to this, other than to say, "You're comparing me to the people of Sodom?"

"No, my boy," Albert laughed. "I'm merely questioning our individualistic view of responsibility. A view, after all, that was discredited the moment it was uttered by its earliest proponent, when the murderer, Cain, attempted to escape responsibility through the utterance, 'Am I my brother's keeper?'[160]

"The answer to that question, of course, is a resounding, 'Yes!' And if it is 'yes,' then we are responsible not only for ourselves but for others as well, just as prophets from the beginning have recognized, as they have said that the blood of the people would come upon their heads if they failed to teach them.[161]

"Because of all this," Albert continued, "we need to become as worried for our fathers' redemption as we are for our own. After all, the scriptures do tell us that '[our fathers] without us cannot be made perfect—neither can we without [them] be made perfect.'[162] And when you think about it, the whole center of the gospel is about a Savior who took the sins of others on his own head. If we are to be like him, it seems that our feelings about responsibility must expand far beyond ourselves."

These words brought to mind something Michael had read once—something he had loved, something he had felt was true. The memory changed his mood. "I need to read something to you, Al," he said. He scrambled to his feet and hurried out of the room.

A couple of minutes later Michael rounded the corner carrying a worn book, its ample pages yellowed with time. He carried it gently, as if cradling a young bird. "This is one of my favorite books," he said, taking his seat again. "I don't even know why, actually, as I find it difficult to read. But there is such deep beauty and wisdom in it. It's Dostoyevsky's *The Brothers Karamazov*. Have you read it?"

"No," Albert shook his head, "I haven't."

"Something I've read that you have not!" Michael exclaimed joyfully. "Let me just sit here and take that in for a moment."

"Careful not to be too long at it, Counselor," Albert smiled, returning the quip, "for it is also written that 'whosoever shall exalt himself shall be abased; and he that shall humble himself shall be exalted.'"[163]

"Fair enough," Michael laughed. "Let me read you what came to mind. In this passage an amazing character named Father Zossima is describing his older brother, Markel, who had died years earlier. Over the final months of his suffering, Markel transformed from youthful petulance to inspiring depth and love. Let me read a little of this to you."

> "Mother, darling," [my brother] would say, "there must be servants and masters, but if so I will be the servant of my servants, the same as they are to me. And another thing, mother, every one of us has sinned against all men, and I more than any."
>
> Mother positively smiled at that, smiled through her tears. "Why, how could you have sinned against all men, more than all? Robbers and murderers have done

that, but what sin have you committed yet, that you hold yourself more guilty than all?"

"Mother, little heart of mine," he said (he had begun using such strange caressing words at that time), "little heart of mine, my joy, believe me, every one is really responsible to all men for all men and for everything. I don't know how to explain it to you, but I feel it is so, painfully even. And how is it we went on living, getting angry and not knowing?" . . .

There was a great deal more I don't remember. I remember I went once into his room when there was no one else there. It was a bright evening, the sun was setting, and the whole room was lighted up. He beckoned me, and I went up to him. He put his hands on my shoulders and looked into my face tenderly, lovingly; he said nothing for a minute, only looked at me like that.

"Well," he said, "run and play now, enjoy life for me too."

I went out then and ran to play. And many times in my life afterwards I remembered even with tears how he told me to enjoy life for him too.[164]

Michael swallowed in an attempt to shrink the knot that was again forming in his throat.

"That's beautiful," Albert said. "Stunning. And true too, isn't it?"

Michael nodded silently.

"We really are responsible to all, for all, just as he said," Albert continued. "And yet also as he said, I can't quite grasp how and why that is. I just know, as you, too, evidently knew when you first read it, that it's true. There are much deeper strains of responsibility at work in the eternities than we normally consider."

Michael nodded again, this time thinking of his father. *Father, dear heart of mine,* he cried within, *my joy, believe me, every one is really responsible to all men for all men and everything. I don't know how to explain it to you, but I feel it is so, painfully even.*

How is it, then, I went on living, getting angry and not knowing?

23

IN THE FOOTSTEPS OF
THE GREAT PROXY

T hat passage reminds me of another," Albert said. "May I
read something to you as well?"

Michael nodded, his head still down. "Please."

Albert picked up the Bible and opened to the book of
Isaiah.

> He is despised and rejected of men; a man of sor-
> rows, and acquainted with grief: and we hid as it were
> our faces from him; he was despised, and we esteemed
> him not.
>
> Surely he hath borne our griefs, and carried our
> sorrows: yet we did esteem him stricken, smitten of
> God, and afflicted. But he was wounded for our

transgressions, he was bruised for our iniquities: the chastisement of our peace was upon him: and with his stripes we are healed.

All we like sheep have gone astray; we have turned every one to his own way; and the Lord hath laid on him the iniquity of us all.[165]

Albert reverently set the book down. "Responsible to all and for all," he repeated. "Seeing that this is precisely how Jesus lived and why he died, how can it be denied, even if it is not fully understood?"

Michael didn't say anything but just sat, pondering.

"But the Savior's example points to at least one implication of this principle for us," Albert continued. "Consider: He bore *our* griefs, and carried *our* sorrows; he was wounded for *our* transgressions and bruised for *our* iniquities; the chastisement of *our* peace was upon him, and the Lord laid on him *the iniquity of us all.*" Albert paused. "Do you notice anything about the way Isaiah characterized Christ's atonement offering?"

Michael slowly raised his head to meet Albert's gaze. "He did everything Isaiah mentioned in our stead—vicariously for us," Michael observed. "That's what you're saying, isn't it? He was a vicarious sacrifice—doing in proxy for us what each of us needed but none of us could have done."

"Yes, Michael. The atonement is the great, central proxy ordinance of time and eternity.[166] All other ordinances are appendages to it.[167] As with the living, the dead, too, needed to have an atonement made for their sins. Jesus did for them and for us what they and we could not do for ourselves. Anyone who believes in the atonement of Christ therefore implicitly believes, whether he knows it or not, in vicarious work for the dead.

"What we in the Church understand, of course, is that in addition to being the central ordinance of redemption, the atonement, and the Lord's own work after his death, set a pattern for our own service both for the living and for the dead. After his death, the Savior went to preach to the spirits in prison, setting in motion a missionary effort among the dead that continues to this day.[168] Since they, too, must accept the terms of the Lord's covenant and be made holy and without spot in order to endure the glory of God, we, following the example of our Lord, do for the dead what they as spirits are unable to do for themselves: we receive each of the necessary saving ordinances on their behalf. They then, as we here, have the opportunity either to accept or reject those beliefs and commitments. This plan was established from the foundation of the world and was apparently understood by members of the early Church, as Paul wrote, 'Else what shall they do which are baptized for the dead, if the dead rise not at all? why are they then baptized for the dead?'"[169]

Michael nodded. "You know," he said, "Dostoyevsky even got something of the spirit of proxy work right. The dying brother, Markel, with no bitterness at all in his voice, told his little brother, 'Run and play now. Enjoy life for me too.'"

"Ah, yes," Albert smiled. "'Enjoy life for me too.' Yes, exactly. 'Live and play and worship as if you were responsible to all and for all, for you truly are.'"

Michael's mind was working on a problem. "Jesus' statement to the scribes and Pharisees makes more sense to me now," he said.

"How do you mean?"

"Dad was ignorant. Did he make mistakes? Yes, big ones. And he paid a dear price. To the extent he passed those sins on to ignorant children, he is responsible as well for their sins. But in my case, I'm not ignorant. I know better. To the extent I know better but nevertheless choose to continue my father's sins, then the responsibility for them is mine—down through the generations even."

"Actually," Albert said, "Jesus seems to be suggesting something even more than that."

Michael's brow furrowed. "What?"

"I think what you said is exactly right when the parents sin willfully. When their sins are in ignorance, however, I read Jesus to be saying that they are not responsible for those sins down the generations, even though the descendants suffer from what the Book of Mormon calls in such cases the 'traditions of the fathers.'[170] In that case, on the contrary, it sounds like Jesus is saying that responsibility for sin can actually travel the other way—not only down but also back up the generations of time—for he said that the scribes and Pharisees would be punished for the sins of their fathers back through time."

"But that doesn't make sense," Michael objected.

"I agree that, if true, it's certainly surprising," Albert said. "But there is a perspective from which it makes perfect sense."

"What perspective would that be?" Michael questioned. "I don't see it."

"It makes divine sense if the fundamental unit in eternity is not the individual but the family."

Michael blinked. The thought was so new to him he didn't even know how to formulate an objection to it. His mind whirled.

Albert pointed at the coffee table between them. "You see that table?"

Michael nodded.

"It is comprised of billions upon billions of tiny atoms, is it not?"

"Yes."

"So what is it that sits between us—countless tiny atoms or a table?"

"Well, both, I suppose."

"But those atoms only have meaning to us in this moment because they are in relation to each other in such a way as to form a table."

Michael thought about it. "I suppose that's right, yes."

"It is the same with us. As we sit here, it is easy to see and experience ourselves as individual atoms of the table, as it were. But if that's all we see, and fail to see the extent to which we exist in relation to one another, we miss the grand picture—the picture I believe the Lord sees as he looks at us."

Michael leaned forward in interest.

"Your actions are never only about you, Michael. If your sins can fall on the heads of your parents, for example, as the scriptures say they can, then your repentance must be able to bless them as well."

"My repentance?" Michael repeated in surprise. "If I repent today, that somehow helps my family?"

"Well, it's obvious how it would help your wife and your children, isn't it?"

Michael nodded.

"In matters of eternity," Albert said, "influence flows both ways through time. One only need ponder the effects of the Lord's atonement to see that is so."

"But how?" Michael wondered aloud.

"Let me read something else for you," Albert said. He opened to the ninety-eighth section of the Doctrine and Covenants. "Listen to this."

> If the children shall repent, or the children's children, and turn to the Lord their God, with all their hearts and with all their might, mind, and strength, and restore for all [the] trespasses wherewith . . . their

fathers have trespassed, or their fathers' fathers, then . . . vengeance shall no more come upon them . . . and [those] trespasses shall never be brought any more as a testimony before the Lord against them.[171]

Albert looked up at Michael. "So you see, even repentance can have vicarious ramifications. As we restore for the sins or trespasses of our fathers, or as we ourselves repent of sins that have been passed down to us from our fathers, it appears that we can help to save our fathers from responsibility they otherwise would have had for suffering caused by their sins. We can make restitution, for example, and restore to aggrieved parties what our fathers, from the spirit world, can no longer restore. Perhaps we can help to put a stop to iniquities they might have put in motion before they passed on. And we certainly can repent of any impure feelings within ourselves that their actions might have invited."

Albert dipped his head and looked thoughtfully at Michael from over the top of his glasses. "Through both proxy work and the work of our own repentance, which itself is a vicarious work, we are 'response-able'—that is, positioned, Michael, and able, to perform a saving labor on behalf of our families.

"Which, by the way, has always been the point of the Lord's labor. Because we are, fundamentally, of one another, there is no such thing as a merely glorified individual; the Lord's purpose is, and has always been, to make you, and me, and us, into a glorified house."[172]

24

THE LORD'S HOUSE

Let me illustrate what I mean through a biblical story. Do you know the history of the two kingdoms of Israel—the kingdom of Israel in the north and the kingdom of Judah in the south?"

"Vaguely."

"Well, the story really begins with King David. After he became king, he expressed to the prophet, Nathan, his desire to build a permanent temple to replace the cloth sanctuary the Israelites had used since their forty years in the desert. That very night, the Lord delivered to Nathan a message for David, a message known as the Davidic covenant. The message was essentially this: 'Don't build me a house to dwell in. Rather, I will build thee a house. I will raise up thy seed after thee, which shall be of thy sons, and I will establish his kingdom. And he shall build me a house, and I will establish his throne for ever.'"[173]

"The Lord was going to build David a house?" Michael asked.

"Not a physical structure. After all, David already dwelt in a splendid home of cedar.[174] Rather, the Lord was making a promise regarding the 'House of David'—that is, the *family* of David. The promise was this: That among David's posterity, a son of God would be raised up who would build the Lord's family or house in the eternities and there rule for evermore."

"That was fulfilled in Christ," Michael said, "who was a descendent of David."

"Exactly," Albert agreed. "Christ came to build the eternal family—a house of people that would, through him, inherit all that the Father hath.[175] These are they of whom Paul declared, 'Ye are God's building'—the house or family of Christ.[176] Paul taught that all who become the children of Christ are accounted the seed of Abraham and heirs of all the promises given to the family of Abraham.[177] We become members of the Church of the Firstborn,[178] his kingdom, his family, his house."

"Wait!" Michael interrupted excitedly. "We become his spiritual house through the power of the ordinances of the Lord's physical house on earth, don't we?"

"Exactly, Michael. And that's a point that is also illustrated by this story."

"How so?"

"David's son, Solomon, built the temple that David had desired to build. And from that moment on, the fortunes of the families of Israel turned on their attitudes toward the temple."

Michael leaned forward. "They did?"

"At Solomon's death," Albert nodded, "the kingdom split into two. Led by a man named Jeroboam, the northern ten tribes of Israel revolted and formed the northern kingdom or 'kingdom of Israel.' The tribes of Judah and Benjamin were left to populate the southern kingdom or 'kingdom of Judah,' which was led by Solomon's son, Rehoboam.

"After Jeroboam led the revolt against Rehoboam, he committed a grievous sin. You see, the temple that Solomon built was located in Jerusalem within the territory of the southern kingdom. By law, the people of Israel were to return to the temple every year to offer up sacrifices for their sins. Jeroboam worried that if his people returned to worship at Jerusalem, they might join once again with their fellows of the tribes of Judah and Benjamin, putting his own kingdom at risk.[179] In order to keep his people from returning to Jerusalem, he set up alternative places of worship in the north—other gods, as it were[180]—that would keep them from the temple.

"This sin of turning away from the temple—what the scriptures refer to as 'the sin of Jeroboam'—was repeated by each of the nineteen kings that followed Jeroboam to the throne of the northern kingdom.[181] Together, these twenty temple-rejecting kings in the north came from five separate houses or families.

Incredibly, each of these houses was destroyed, finally culminating in the destruction of all of the houses within the kingdom when the northern kingdom was captured and carried away captive by Assyria in 721 B.C."

"So the families of those who turned from the temple were destroyed," Michael observed. "They did not continue."

"Yes, Michael, a lesson that was mirrored in the southern kingdom as well."

"But they had a temple in their midst," Michael replied.

"Yes, and so do we. But are our hearts turned toward it? Do we reverence and frequent it as we should?"

Michael bowed his head.

"That is the question for us, isn't it?" Albert asked. "You see, despite the temple being in their midst, of the twenty kings that ruled the southern kingdom of Judah until it was captured and carried away captive by the Babylonians in 587 B.C., all but four erected false gods and turned their people away from the temple. The righteousness of the other four—Asa, Jehoshaphat, Hezekiah, and Josiah—consisted precisely in their breaking down the altars of false gods that their predecessors had erected and returning their people to the house of the Lord.[182] In each case, however, later kings again turned the people away from the temple. Warnings from the prophets went unheeded, and the result was an end to the southern kingdom as well.

"We know from the Book of Mormon that the Lord preserved a remnant of that people unto himself and led them to a

It is significant, I would suggest to you, that he merely an individual in that case, but an entire family. Book of Mormon, too, unfolds as the story of families with the tragic destruction of an entire house."

Albert looked at Michael. "Think about what we talked about on Monday. When the younger son in the parable finally recognized his brokenness, the Lord did not renew him in the solitary country to which he had journeyed. Rather, he conveyed him home. Home to a father he had abandoned and likely hurt and to a brother whose hurt remained. Does that sound familiar? Do not our own family stories hearken to that one?"

Michael breathed in deeply and nodded.

"And then the father took the returning son into his house—not as a servant, which is all the son thought he deserved, but as a son.[183]

"But what of the one who remained outside? If the returned prodigal, like Dostoyevsky's Markel, can stay in the middle of the humble realization that he is responsible to all and for all and join his father's efforts in reaching out to the brother, he will become a tool in the Lord's hands in that family—a healer of the breach, a savior on mount Zion, one through whom the entire family can enter the Father's house and be redeemed."[184]

"But what a heavy role to play," Michael said, head still bowed.

"It would be heavy, wouldn't it, if there was not One who

has already taken upon himself every burden. For us, then, to carry others' burdens is merely to accept a yoke that has already been carried. It is a burden, when we accept it, that is exactly the opposite of heavy. The heavy burden is the burden of denying responsibility for the pain we and others feel and cause. The burden of claiming responsibility, which is a burden the Lord has already carried, is the lightest thing in the Heavens."

Michael raised his head, eyes wide with realization. He opened *The Brothers Karamazov* again and read to himself something more about Markel.

> The windows of his room looked out into the garden, and our garden was a shady one, with old trees in it which were coming into bud. The first birds of spring were flitting in the branches, chirruping and singing at the windows. Looking at them and admiring them, [Markel] began suddenly begging their forgiveness too. "Birds of heaven, happy birds, forgive me, for I have sinned against you too." None of us could understand that at the time, but he shed tears of joy. "Yes," he said, "there was such a glory of God all about me; birds, trees, meadows, sky, only I lived in shame and dishonoured it all and did not notice the beauty and glory."
>
> "You take too many sins on yourself," mother used to say, weeping.
>
> "Mother, darling, it's for joy, not for grief I am

crying. Though I can't explain it to you, I like to humble myself before them, for I don't know how to love them enough."[185]

Michael looked up. *It's for joy, not for grief!* He realized that to feel responsible for another is no burden. Since it's the truth, as Markel discovered, it is the only freeing belief.[186] Rest before the Lord is possible only when we lay down the hard labor of convincing ourselves otherwise.

Michael smiled and set the book down. This wasn't just about his father. His marriage with Angie, civil as it was, was hardly celestial. And his children—did he really know them? Did he know their hearts—what they liked and what they didn't? Were they on his mind? Did he feel about them as Markel came to feel about the birds that blessed his life?

He thought as well about his brother and sister. They had been so much better toward their father than he himself had been. Did they know how much he appreciated them—how much he wished he could have been like them?

His thoughts then turned to his father's father, and all who came before him. Had he ever considered their lives? They who spent their lives constructing the family circumstances into which Michael himself had been born—did he ever feel grateful to, and responsible for, them? Had his heart ever turned toward them in appreciation, concern, and love?

He looked at Albert. *Such a toweringly gentle soul!* And then it struck Michael that the titles we use for others within the

Church have a more significant meaning than he'd ever considered. We call each other "brother" and "sister"; we are to be family—siblings within the family of Christ. The ideas Albert had been talking about in terms of our responsibility for family members through time were not limited to blood relations. Through Christ's blood, we are all related to one another, united through his blood in *Him*.

Michael's eyes started to water. Every moment with Albert had been a Sabbath; every room a holy place. "Thank you, Brother Al. Words can't express. All I have done is receive. You have only given."

Wrinkles spread from the corners of Albert's eyes to his temples. "What a blessing it is to be wrong in such a generous way," he said. "To this lone, expiring soul, your presence has been a gift beyond measure, Michael. I will be forever grateful." Then he added, "But may I add one point to what we've discussed?"

"Please," Michael said.

"Although others are blessed through our service in the temple, like all unfeigned service, temple service blesses the giver most of all. For where all is service, there you find a spirit more pure and sanctifying than any in all the earth. The temple is truly the Lord's holy space on earth, and to frequent it as much as circumstances allow is to bathe in his holiness and to become prepared for his light." Albert's eyes gazed gently at Michael. "I might choose a lot of words to describe that experience, Michael," he said, "but 'boring' would never be one of them."

Michael looked down. How shallow he had been!

"However, I need to *go* to and *experience* the temple," Albert continued, "in order to be blessed with love for it. As interesting as it might be to ponder the temple through the scriptures as we have been doing, for example, in order to *love* it, I must experience the temple itself. Likewise, in order to love the Sabbath, I must begin to take the Sabbath itself seriously—as a 'perpetual covenant'[187] with the Lord. A love for, and testimony of, each of the mediums of holiness cannot be acquired by proxy.[188] We learn to love the scriptures by conversing with them; we discover love for the Sabbath as we strive to keep it holy; we cherish the temple as we seek out that holy place."

As Michael pondered how shallow he had been, he was struck by another thought. It wasn't simply that he hadn't gone deep enough. It was rather that he had grown accustomed to wading in pools that had no depth to begin with. A turn toward holiness would be a turn toward a different kind of life altogether—to a life where different things mattered than had mattered in the past. Did he desire such a life? He knew that of all questions, this was the most important. 'If ye can no more than desire,'[189] he remembered from the scriptures, then the Lord can take that first offering of will and redeem it into a miracle.

"What's next for you?" Albert asked.

Michael pondered the question, and in the silence the vision of a small home came to his mind.

"There's yet another house I need to visit," he said.

25

A HOME RENEWED

M ichael took Interstate 95 northeast up the Connecticut coast. Normally, he would have had the window down, his hair whipping in the breeze of Long Island Sound. Today, however, he wanted quiet. The only sound in the cabin was the purr of the efficient climate control system.

At New Haven, he veered north onto Interstate 91. A couple of miles later he exited eastbound onto Foxon Boulevard. Although less than an hour from his own place in Stamford, it had been years since he had driven this road.

In a few minutes, a small weathered sign pointed Michael to his destination: Totoket Valley Mobile Home Park. Like the prodigal many years away, Michael was finally returning home. He turned his car onto the narrow lane. Three quarters of the way down on the left he saw the back of his father's 1974

Chevy Impala stretching out of its stall and into the street. There was no room in the space for Michael. He parked on the lane.

The tiny strip of grass in front of his father's home was shaggy with neglect. Michael felt a tinge of guilt, as it had never occurred to him to lend a hand. A ten-foot skiff with a small outboard motor was parked where the front of his father's car should have been. This small boat was perhaps his father's most cherished possession, as he spent countless hours fishing from it on a nearby lake. Michael supposed it was his father's only positive diversion. The rusted ball on the back of the Impala's bumper told him it had been many months, if not years, since the boat had been used.

A sign by the door read, *Too Late to Turn Back Now. Try to Make the Best of It.* Michael touched the sign and smiled. He had always thought it a pathetic way to welcome a guest. Today he found humor in it.

The door was ajar, as it had been for as many years as Michael could remember. He pulled to open it, but the door caught on the bottom. *Oh yeah,* he thought, as he tugged to release it.

Having negotiated the door, he stepped up into the home, a home his father hadn't been back to since his second leg was amputated two months earlier. Michael shuffled around, not looking for anything in particular. Truth was, he didn't have many memories of this place, despite it being his father's home for the last fifteen years. He didn't even know why he was here. Just wanted a connection somehow, a connection he only first felt on the last night of his father's life.

Michael was surprised to find that the home was mostly tidy. He wandered into the bedroom. The bed was even made! He didn't know why this struck him so. Perhaps because he himself had not made a bed in years. He looked through the books on the nightstand. Louis L'Amour. *That figures,* he thought. *Fishing* magazine. That, too, seemed obvious. But other titles surprised him: *The Five Love Languages,* a two-volume biography of Winston Churchill, and, most surprising of all, a Gideon Bible. *Probably pilfered it from a motel room.* The dig came so easily to him. He dropped his head in shame. *Dear Father,* he cried within, *please help me to love and honor my father.*

He turned to leave the bedroom, and then he saw it. Staring back at him was a collage of pictures of Michael beginning from the time he was a small child. He walked slowly forward and reached out to touch them, caressing the pictures of himself in wonder. Tears streamed down his cheeks, his eyes so full of water he could barely make out the photos. In one, he was proudly displaying a fish for the picture taker—his father, he remembered. His young eyes beamed at the man behind the camera. In another, he was waving at his father as he walked victoriously off the court after a hard-fought high school basketball game. In another he was an infant in his mother's arms.

The tears now dripped from his chin. He shuddered and

leaned against the wall to steady himself. *Mom! I've barely thought about Mom!* His chest heaved.

Memories now came in torrents. He remembered the park down the street from the house of his youth. His parents took him there often. He remembered his mother on the other end of the teeter-totter and the hands of his father pushing him to go higher on the swing. He remembered the walks home, his parents arm-in-arm, smiling and laughing, his mother leaning her head on his father's shoulder. *She loved him!* he realized. How had he forgotten so? *I've dishonored her, too, in my dishonoring of him.* He looked heavenward again. "I'm so sorry!" he cried aloud. "Please Lord, I'm so sorry." He shook his head and shuddered anew. "Please forgive me, Lord. Please—Mom, Dad—please forgive me."

He took in a deep breath and wiped at his eyes. He turned again and scanned the photos. He was about to pass out of the room when his eyes fell on the farthest photo to the right. He froze as he looked at it. Blinking, he wiped at his eyes again to clear his sight.

It was a picture of himself disembarking from his flight at JFK upon returning home from his mission. In the photo, he, like another young man who had long been away from home, was being swallowed up in a welcoming, tearful embrace. The joy of the memory of that day swept over him. He looked closer at the picture, trying to make out who was hugging him. When he did, he was overcome with emotion and collapsed to the floor.

Somehow, over the years, he had forgotten.

The embrace was his father's.

NOTES

1. See Moses 6:59.
2. Moses 6:59.
3. See Alma 12:24; 34:32; 42:10, 13.
4. See Isaiah 57:15; Moses 6:57; 7:35.
5. 1 Nephi 2:4.
6. 1 Nephi 3:16.
7. See Luke 18:22.
8. Jeffrey R. Holland, "Daddy, Donna, and Nephi," *Ensign*, September 1976, 7.
9. 1 Nephi 1:9–12.
10. 1 Nephi 1:15, 18.
11. See 1 Nephi 1:12.
12. See 2 Nephi 32:3.
13. 2 Corinthians 3:14.
14. See 3 Nephi 12:24.
15. Mosiah 1:7.
16. See Mosiah 1:9–18.

17. Mosiah 2:4.
18. See Mosiah 2:5–6.
19. Mosiah 2:9.
20. See Mosiah 2:10–24.
21. Mosiah 2:24–26, 32–33.
22. See Mosiah 2:32–33.
23. Mosiah 2:38.
24. See Luke 15:11–32.
25. See Luke 15:1–3.
26. See Luke 15:29.
27. See Romans 3:10, 23.
28. See Luke 15:22–23.
29. See Luke 15:31.
30. See, for example, Ezekiel 36:26.
31. See Ether 3:2.
32. See Mosiah 3:17; 16:5; Alma 42:10; Ether 3:2; 1 Corinthians 2:14.
33. Alma 42:24.
34. D&C 101:22–24.
35. D&C 112:23.
36. See 2 Nephi 9:10–12; Alma 12:16; Alma 40:26; Alma 42:9; D&C 29:41.
37. JST Exodus 33:20.
38. D&C 88:22; emphasis added; Moses 6:57; emphasis added. Joseph Smith taught that "God himself dwells in eternal fire; flesh and blood cannot go there, for all corruption is devoured by the fire. Our God is consuming fire" (*Teachings of the Prophet Joseph Smith*, compiled by Joseph Fielding Smith [Salt Lake City: Deseret Book, 1976], 367).
39. 2 Thessalonians 2:8; Malachi 3:2.
40. See Alma 7:11–13.
41. See 3 Nephi 11:14–15.

42. Ephesians 5:30.
43. Isaiah 53:5.
44. D&C 60:7.
45. See D&C 93:30–32.
46. See Numbers 21:4–9.
47. See Helaman 8:14–15.
48. Mosiah 1:11.
49. Mosiah 4:1–7.
50. Galatians 3:24.
51. 3 Nephi 12:19.
52. See Mosiah 4:2.
53. See Mosiah 5:2.
54. See 1 Nephi 3:7.
55. 3 Nephi 12:21; see also Matthew 5:21.
56. 3 Nephi 12:22; see also Matthew 5:22.
57. D&C 1:31.
58. See Moroni 7:42; D&C 60:7.
59. 3 Nephi 12:27; see also Matthew 5:27.
60. 3 Nephi 12:28–30; see also Matthew 5:28–30.
61. See Matthew 18:35; Alma 5:29; 1 Corinthians 13:1–13; Moroni 7:44–48; Matthew 5:5, 7; 3 Nephi 12:5, 7; Exodus 20:12.
62. Romans 5:20; 3:19.
63. Alma 42:17–18.
64. See Alma 34:14.
65. Romans 3:28.
66. Romans 3:31.
67. Ether 12:27; Isaiah 51:7; Romans 2:15; 2 Nephi 8:7.
68. 2 Nephi 2:5–7.
69. Romans 5:20; 3:19.
70. See 2 Nephi 2:23.
71. See 2 Nephi 2:13; Alma 42:17.

72. See Genesis 3:15; Moses 4:21.
73. See David A. Bednar, "Clean Hands and a Pure Heart," *Ensign*, Nov. 2007, 80–83.
74. See Moroni 10:33.
75. See Joseph Fielding Smith, "The Plan of Salvation," *Ensign*, Nov. 1971, 3.
76. Isaiah 1:18; Mosiah 5:2.
77. D&C 77:12.
78. See Genesis 2:2–7; Moses 3:2–7; Abraham 5:2–7.
79. See D&C 84:24; Hebrews 4:10–11; Jacob 1:7; Alma 12:33–34; 3 Nephi 27:19.
80. Hebrews 4:10.
81. Hebrews 4:11.
82. Boyd K. Packer, "The Pattern of Our Parentage," *Ensign,* Nov. 1984, 66; Dallin H. Oaks, "Pornography," *Ensign*, May 2005, 87.
83. Alma 37:34.
84. D&C 59:8–12.
85. See Exodus 20:11.
86. See D&C 20:77, 79.
87. Mosiah 4:2.
88. Luke 15:12.
89. Alma 11:38.
90. Alma 11:39–40.
91. Mosiah 16:15.
92. See 2 Nephi 31:12–13.
93. Moroni 8:26; see Mosiah 5:2.
94. Ether 3:14.
95. Mosiah 5:7.
96. Isaiah 9:6.
97. Mosiah 5:2.
98. See Mosiah 5:11–12.

99. Exodus 31:13.
100. See Titus 3:5; Exodus 31:17.
101. James 2:10.
102. See 2 Nephi 4:32.
103. See 1 Nephi 4:6.
104. See D&C 50:17–18.
105. See Matthew 12:1–8.
106. Matthew 11:28–29.
107. 3 Nephi 12:23–24.
108. Mosiah 4:2.
109. See Helaman 12:7–8.
110. Romans 3:27.
111. See Romans 3:19.
112. See Mosiah 4:19.
113. See Isaiah 56:4–5, 7.
114. D&C 38:8.
115. See Moroni 6:4.
116. See 2 Nephi 32:3.
117. See Alma 13:30.
118. See 2 Nephi 25:23; Moroni 6:4.
119. See Alma 24:11.
120. See Alma 24:11; David A. Bednar, "Clean Hands and a Pure Heart," *Ensign,* Nov. 2007, 80–83.
121. See Neal A. Maxwell, "Swallowed Up in the Will of the Father," *Ensign,* Nov. 1995, 24; 3 Nephi 9:20.
122. Brigham Young, in *Journal of Discourses,* 26 vols. (London: Latter-day Saints' Book Depot, 1854–86), 3:47.
123. Ether 12:27.
124. See Isaiah 28:10, 13; 2 Nephi 28:30.
125. See D&C 132:4, 6.
126. See D&C 84:32–33.

127. See D&C 132:7.

128. See D&C 132:4, 6.

129. See Malachi 4:4–6; Joseph Smith—History 1:37–39.

130. April 3, 1836, just happened to be the eve of the Passover, when Jews the world over were keeping a traditional empty chair at the table of their respective Seder feasts in invitation for Elijah to return in accordance with Malachi's prophecy.

131. See D&C 110:13–16.

132. Malachi 3:7.

133. Malachi 3:7.

134. See D&C 84:32–33.

135. See D&C 107:18–19.

136. D&C 84:19–25.

137. See Genesis 5:24; Moses 7:18–21.

138. See JST Genesis 14: 27, 32–36; Hebrews 7:8.

139. Joseph Smith, *The Words of Joseph Smith*, compiled and edited by Andrew F. Ehat and Lyndon Cook (Provo, Utah: BYU Religious Studies Center, 1980), 9.

140. See JST Genesis 14:34.

141. D&C 132:4.

142. Brigham Young in *Journal of Discourses*, 3:47.

143. For the Lord's instructions to Moses regarding the temple, see Exodus 25–30.

144. See D&C 107:18–19.

145. D&C 84:19–22.

146. The passage can seem ambiguous as to whether it is saying that one must have received the ordinances of the holy priesthood or have the power of godliness in order to see the face of God and live. However, since it says that the power of godliness is not manifest unto man without the ordinances, it reduces to the same

point: One must have received the ordinances of the holy priesthood in order to survive the glory of the Father.

147. See *The Words of Joseph Smith*, 120.

148. See D&C 93:12–14; 76:76–77.

149. See D&C 84:24.

150. D&C 84:24–25.

151. D&C 13; see D&C 84:19, 26; 107:18–20.

152. D&C 84:33, 35–40.

153. D&C 84:35.

154. See Bruce R. McConkie, *A New Witness for the Articles of Faith* (Salt
Lake City: Deseret Book, 1985), 646–49; Joseph Fielding Smith,
Church History and Modern Revelation (Salt Lake City: Deseret
Book, 1947), 2:64–65.

155. Joseph Smith—History 1:39.

156. See Matthew 23:27.

157. See Matthew 23:23–29.

158. Matthew 23:29–30, 34–35; JST Matthew 23:36.

159. See, for example, 2 Nephi 4:5–6; Jacob 3:10; Mosiah 29:31.

160. Genesis 4:9.

161. See Mosiah 2:27–28; 2 Nephi 9:44; Ether 12:38.

162. See D&C 128:15; Hebrews 11:40.

163. Matthew 23:12.

164. Fyodor Dostoyevsky, *The Brothers Karamazov* (New York: Random
House, 1943), 344–45.

165. Isaiah 53:3–6.

166. See Gordon B. Hinckley, "The Great Things Which God Has
Revealed," *Ensign*, May 2005, 80.

167. See *Teachings of the Prophet Joseph Smith*, 121.

168. See 1 Peter 3:19; D&C 138.

169. 1 Corinthians 15:29; see D&C 124:33–34; 128:5–9.

170. See Mosiah 3:11. (Jesus' blood atones for the sins of those who did not know the will of God.)
171. D&C 98:47–48.
172. See, for example, 2 Samuel 7:11; 1 Chronicles 17:10; Hebrews 3:6; 1 Peter 2:5.
173. See 1 Chronicles 17:4–6, 10–14.
174. See 1 Chronicles 17:1.
175. See D&C 84:38.
176. 1 Corinthians 3:9; see Hebrews 3:6.
177. See Galatians 3:26–29.
178. See D&C 76:54, 71, 94, 102; 78:21; 88:5; 93:22; 107:19; Hebrews 12:23.
179. See 1 Kings 12:26–27.
180. See 1 Kings 12:28–29.
181. See, for example, 1 Kings 15:26, 34; 16:19, 25–26, 30–31; 22:52–53; 2 Kings 3:2–3; 10:31; 13:2, 11; 14:24; 15:9, 18, 24, 28; 17:2–23.
182. See passages regarding Asa in 2 Chronicles 14–16, Jehoshaphat in 2 Chronicles 17–20, Hezekiah in 2 Chronicles 29–32 and 2 Kings 18–19, and Josiah in 2 Chronicles 34–35 and 2 Kings 22–23.
183. See Luke 15:19, 21, 24.
184. See Luke 15:28–32; Isaiah 58:12; Obadiah 1:21.
185. Dostoyevsky, *The Brothers Karamazov*, 345.
186. See John 8:32.
187. See Exodus 31:16.
188. See Douglas C. Callister, "Knowing That We Know," *Ensign*, Nov. 2007, 100–101.
189. See Alma 32:27.